Exploring Florida's Atlantic Coast Beaches

Help Us Keep This Guide Up to Date

Every effort has been made by the authors and editors to make this guide as accurate and useful as possible. However, many things can change after a guide is published—trails are rerouted, regulations change, techniques evolve, facilities come under new management, etc.

We would love to hear from you concerning your experiences with this guide and how you feel it could be improved and kept up to date. While we may not be able to respond to all comments and suggestions, we'll take them to heart and we'll also make certain to share them with the author. Please send your comments and suggestions to the following address:

The Globe Pequot Press
Reader Response/Editorial Department
P.O. Box 480
Guilford, CT 06437

Or you may e-mail us at:
editorial@globe-pequot.com

Thanks for your input, and happy travels!

A FALCON GUIDE®

Exploring Florida's Atlantic Coast Beaches

Including the Florida Keys

George Hurchalla

FALCON®

GUILFORD, CONNECTICUT
HELENA, MONTANA

AN IMPRINT OF THE GLOBE PEQUOT PRESS

A FALCON GUIDE®

Text design: Nancy Freeborn
Photo credits: All photos are by the author unless otherwise noted.
Maps by Stefanie Ward © The Globe Pequot Press.

Library of Congress Cataloging-in-Publication Data.

Hurchalla, George.
Exploring Florida's Atlantic coast beaches : including the Florida Keys / George Hurchalla.—1st ed.
p. cm.
Includes index.
ISBN 0-7627-2470-6
1. Atlantic Coast (Fla.)—Guidebooks. 2. Beaches—Florida— Atlantic Coast—Guidebooks. 3. Florida Keys (Fla.)—Guidebooks. I. Title.

F317.A74 H87 2002
917.59404'64—dc21

2002032518

Manufactured in the United States of America
First Edition/First Printing

The prices and rates listed in this guidebook were confirmed at press time. We recommend, however, that you call establishments to obtain current information before traveling.

Acknowledgments

My mother and father—for their love and support
Ross Witham—for the turtles
Florida state parks—for doing such a fine job of preserving old Florida
Jan Godown for passing this book my way
The Atlantic Ocean—for all the surf, fish, and lobster
All the citizens of Florida who fought to preserve and expand public beach access

Locator Map by Region

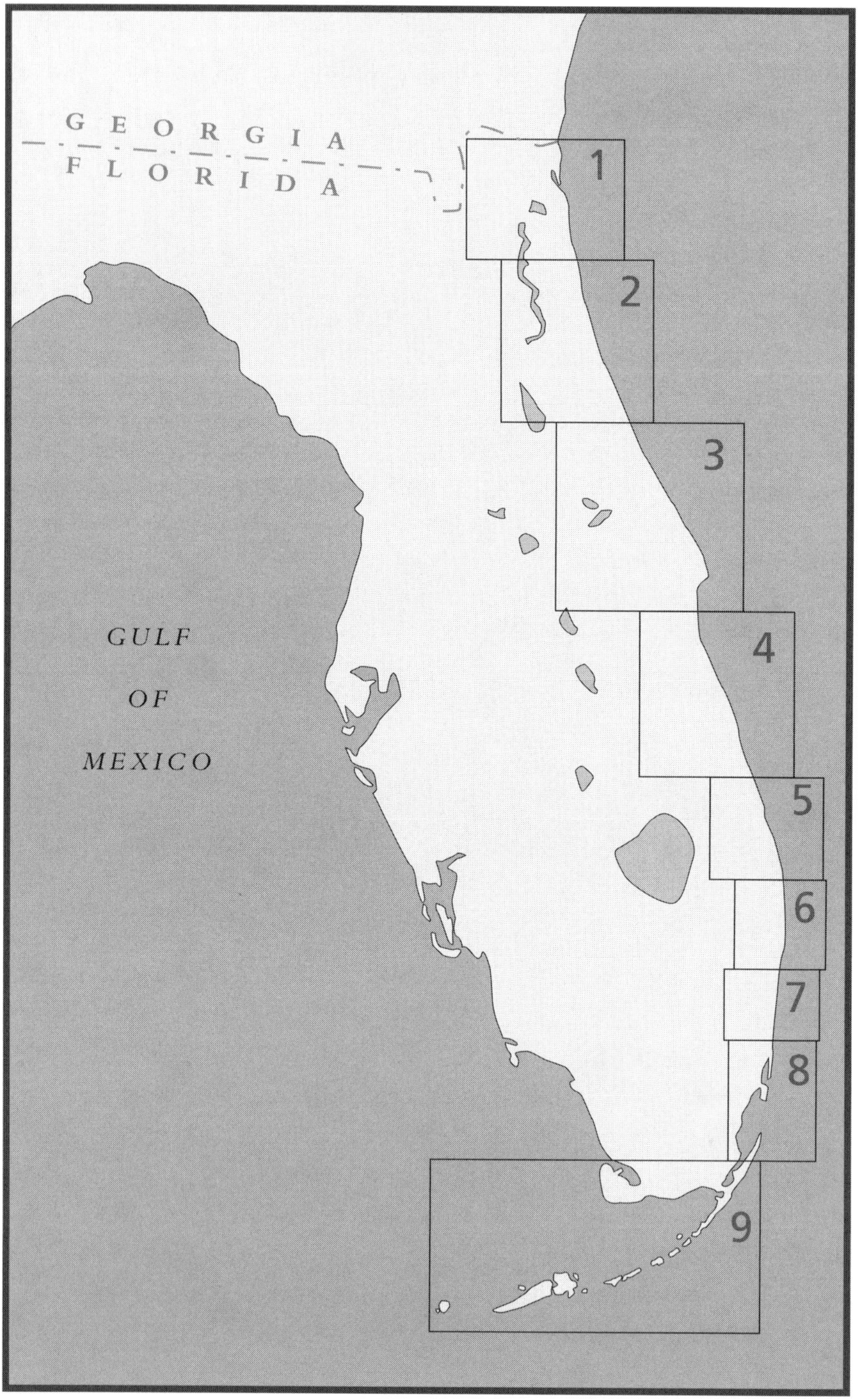

Contents

The Sunshine State xi
How to Use This Guide xiii

Region 1 1
Fort Clinch State Park 5
American Beach 7
Amelia Island State Park 8
Big Talbot Island State Park 9
Little Talbot Island State Park 11
Huguenot Memorial Park/Fort George Island 12
Hanna Park 14
Guana River State Park 15
The Town of Eight Flags 18

Region 2 19
Anastasia State Park 23
Frank Butler Park 24
Fort Matanzas National Monument 25
Washington Oaks State Gardens aka The Rocks 27
Gamble Rogers Memorial State Recreation Area at Flagler Beach 29
Oceanfront Park 30
Bicentennial Park 31
Daytona Beach 32
Lighthouse Point Park 34
The Turtle Man 37

Region 3 39
Smyrna Dunes Park 45
Bethune Beach Park 47
Apollo Beach—Canaveral National Seashore North 48
Playalinda Beach—Canaveral National Seashore South 50
Jetty Park 51
Cherie Down Park 52
Canaveral Pier/Cocoa Beach 53
Lori Wilson Park 54
Patrick Air Force Base 55
Shuttle Launches 57

Region 4 59
Pelican Beach Park. 64
Indialantic Boardwalk. 65
Spessard Holland Park. 66
Long Point Park 67
Sebastian Inlet State Park, North Side 69
Sebastian Inlet State Park, South Side 71
Jaycee Park 72
South Beach Park 73
Avalon. 74
Pepper Beach County Park 75
Fort Pierce Inlet State Park 76
Beach Walk 78

Region 5 81
Frederick Douglass Beach 85
Walton Rocks Beach/Turtle Creek Beach 87
Jensen Public Beach aka Sea Turtle Beach 88
Stuart Beach 89
Bathtub Reef Beach 90
St. Lucie Inlet State Preserve 93
Hobe Sound National Wildlife Refuge 95
Hobe Sound Public Beach 97
Blowing Rocks Preserve 98
Coral Cove Beach 99
The Shipwrecked Quaker 100

Region 6 103
Carlin Park 108
Juno Beach Park/Loggerhead Park 110
John D. MacArthur Beach State Park 111
Ocean Reef Park 113
Riviera Beach Municipal Beach 114
Reef Road 115
Phipps Ocean Park 116
Lake Worth Municipal Beach/Kreusler Park 117
Ocean Ridge Hammock Park 119
Delray Beach 120
Gulfstream Park 121
Red Reef Park 123
South Inlet Park 124
The Stream 125

Region 7 127
Deerfield Beach 133
Pompano Beach 134
Hugh Taylor Birch State Park 135
Fort Lauderdale Beach 136
John U. Lloyd State Park 138
North Beach Park 139
Hollywood Beach 140
Haulover Beach 142
Wreck Diving 143

Region 8 145
North Shore Open Space Park 150
65th Street Beach 151
South Beach 151
Virginia Key Beach 153
Crandon Park Beach 154
Cape Florida/Bill Baggs State Park 156
Matheson Hammock Beach Park 159
Biscayne National Park 160
The South Beach Scene 162

Region 9 163
Cannon Beach/John Pennekamp State Park 168
Bahia Honda State Park 170
Fort Zachary Taylor 171
County Beach/Key West 172
Dry Tortugas National Park 174
Hurricanes 175

Index 177
About the Author 184

The Sunshine State

At one time or another throughout history, all of Florida has been a beach. During cyclical melting of the polar ice caps, the entire state was underwater up to the beginnings of the Appalachians. Sometimes the narrow central ridge, the only "high" land of the state, was lapped by waves. At other times the water receded and the state widened considerably. The east coast dropped off sharply to the Gulf Stream, much as Palm Beach does today, but the coast expanded much farther to the east up at Daytona Beach and Jacksonville. At the southern tip, the oolitic limestone of the Florida Keys was pushed upward by volcanic activity in the Caribbean. Coral reefs grew in dramatic fashion atop it.

In the past century Florida has been reshaped greatly by humans. Yet nature has struck back with staggering force. The 1928 hurricane destroyed the fledgling Lake Okeechobee dike, drowning the Palm Beaches, while the incomprehensible force of the 1935 hurricane obliterated the railroad and everything in its path in the Florida Keys. Hurricane Andrew in 1992 devastated the southern reaches of Miami, and powerful winter storms called "northeasters" reshape the beaches annually. The fluidity of Florida's coastline is a marvel.

The attraction of Florida is that it can be so many things to so many people. It is a constantly evolving landscape, 426 miles long from Georgia to Key West, with roughly 580 miles of beaches. The Seminole Indians only came to the state in the early 1800s, a mixture of tribes displaced from northern regions by Europeans and driven south to make their final undefeated stand in the Everglades. All history in Florida is recent history. In Florida it is never possible to be more than 75 miles from a beach, and 90 percent of the population lives within 10 miles of the ocean! The possibilities for the beachgoer are limitless, from the wildest party beaches to seemingly endless tracts of wilderness strands without another soul.

How to Use This Book

Exploring Florida's Atlantic Coast Beaches is a comprehensive guide to the best beaches of the east coast of Florida and the Florida Keys. Separated into nine regions, beginning at Fernandina Beach by the Georgia border and ending in the far southwestern islands of the Dry Tortugas, the regions can be identified on the overview map of the state (see page iv). Within each region, maps point out the location of each of the area beaches.

An introduction to the region begins each section, giving an overview of the area and differentiating the types of beaches. Local history and other highlights are mentioned. Access directions to the region from major highways are given. The beaches of the region are listed in north-to-south order, followed by a list of area campsites. The "Other Points of Interest" section details historic sites, museums, zoos, and places of natural wonder close to the beach.

At the end of each section, there are informative essays on a variety of subjects, ranging from local characters to history to creatures of the beach and marine environment.

Beach Safety and Etiquette

Don't kick sand in people's faces! Okay, that's a little too obvious. While beach experiences are generally safe, there are a variety of dangers that you can easily avoid. First, there's harmful critters. Strong onshore winds blow in the Portuguese man-of-war, a deadly jellyfish with a floating blue sac and long tentacles. Give them a wide berth in the ocean, and don't touch them on the beach. Sea turtles love them, so the more turtles we have around, the less we have to worry. Sea lice are another concern. Tiny stinging particles, broken jellyfish tentacles, or larval jellyfish, can make some people erupt in painful rashes. See what lifeguard-posted beach condition signs say about whether they're around. Sharks are not a concern along most of the east coast, but special care should be taken during the baitfish migration in autumn months, especially in Brevard and Volusia Counties. Florida is the shark attack capital of the world and has gotten a lot of publicity in recent years, but that's no cause for panic. The numbers reflect the extraordinary numbers of beachgoers in Florida and the stubbornness of surfers—I'm guilty—in staying out in the water while surrounded by baitfish and sharks. Virtually none of the attacks is fatal, and most are committed by sharks less than 4 feet long. Most attacks occur in the muddier waters of the northern beaches; they're relatively rare in the clear waters of South Florida and the Keys.

Opposite page: There's something for everyone on Florida's Atlantic Coast.

On the beach, humans have to share the sand with vehicles in some of the counties above Canaveral National Seashore, including Volusia, Flagler, and Duval. Make sure you set down your towel well clear of the paths most vehicles travel along the beach. The Atlantic can kick up dangerous surf anywhere north of Miami, and rip currents have to be watched for anytime there is a lot of swell. These dangerous currents will pull you out to sea—don't fight them, but swim *across* them until you're free of their pull—and there will always be warnings posted about them at guarded beaches.

As far as interacting with other humans, it's mostly a case of live-and-let-live. There is one official nude beach, at Haulover Beach, where gawkers will be escorted away. At unofficial ones, like on some wilderness beaches, just be aware that when humans are more than a mile away from other humans they have a propensity to shed their clothes. If this has been a subject of controversy or arrests at any given beach, I mention it.

Beach Ecology

Where natural sand dunes have been left intact (which is most of the Florida coast outside of major urban areas), a protected plant called the sea oat is one of the most important parts of a stable beach. These long stalks wave gently in the breeze, and their roots provide the only resistance beaches have to ero-

Sea oats protect the dunes from erosion.

sion. In many places the casuarina, or Australian pine, is a common sight along the coast, and over time people have mistakenly associated it as part of old Florida. It is not a native plant, and efforts are being made at most state parks to steadily eradicate it, replacing it with sea grapes and other native species. Hurricane Andrew did this in one fell swoop at Cape Florida, knocking over the park's entire population of Australian pines.

Coquina rock comes and goes in beautiful formations between Jupiter and St. Augustine, an ancient type of rock that was used by the Spanish to construct the oldest fort in Florida, Castillo de San Marcos. In the Florida Keys, beaches are rare because almost all the land is lime rock. On the Gulf beaches, rock is noticeably absent except in human-made structures, which is why the sands shift so dramatically.

Sea turtles make their nests on all Florida beaches in summer months; after enduring years of decline, their numbers are steadily coming back. Raccoons, possums, and bobcats forage along the beach at night, and egrets, blue herons, sandpipers, and ibis hunt for morsels—like sand fleas and ghost crabs—at the water's edge during the day. In parts of the Panhandle, endangered beach mice scurry about the dunes. While at first glance the beach is no more than an expanse of sand, in fact it supports a fascinating and complex ecosystem.

Sea turtles nest on Florida beaches in the summer months. PHOTO: NELIA M. COYLE

Region 1

As you come across the Georgia border, Amelia Island is the first section of coast that welcomes you to Florida. As an introduction to Florida beaches, it's a great start. The historic town of Fernandina sits at the north end, dating back to times of pirates and lawlessness in the frontier era of the various countries colonizing Florida. Fort Clinch, a Civil War–era fort, is a state park that encompasses wide swaths of beautiful beach, woods, marsh, and many other attractions. A cross-state railroad ran from Fernandina to Cedar Key in the latter part of the nineteenth century, the brainchild of state senator David Levy Yulee, and that explains the appearance of his name in small forgotten communities on both coasts. The Peter Fonda film about a North Florida beekeeper, *Ulee's Gold*, owes its name to him. More recently, the John Sayles movie *Sunshine State* was filmed on Amelia Island.

Down the island, the tiny black community of American Beach has played a more recent role in the area's history. For forty years it was a safe haven and resort for ordinary folks and black celebrities throughout the country and now is a quiet town struggling to maintain its identity amid pressures of development. On both sides of Nassau Sound, the only wild, untamed, natural inlet on the east coast of Florida, there are state park beaches, one with a horseback riding concession. The next state park to the south, Little Talbot Island, contains miles and miles of pristine, sandy Atlantic playground. These parks make up the Talbot Islands GeoPark, a unique ecosystem within Florida. They are the last sea islands in the chain that stretches up the whole coast of Georgia.

On the north side of the St. John's River near Jacksonville, the Huguenot Memorial Park occupies a huge peninsula of wild beaches and great fishing opportunities. On the south side, Hanna Park is another great county park developed with countless recreational opportunities. South of Jacksonville Beach, the coast stays private through Ponte Vedra for many miles before you arrive at Guana River State Park, another great public area of vast wetlands and untrammeled beaches.

Access

From the north, take exit 129 east from I–95, following A1A to Fernandina Beach.

From the south, take exit 95 east from I–95 to US 1, jog south, and follow signs to A1A north and Vilano Beach.

Beaches

Fort Clinch State Park
American Beach
Amelia Island State Park
Big Talbot Island State Park
Little Talbot Island State Park
Huguenot Memorial Park/Fort George Island
Hanna Park
Guana River State Park

Camping

Fort Clinch State Park—(904) 277–7274. Sixty-two campsites, beach camp and river camp, hot and cold showers, rest rooms, laundry, vending machines, newspapers, dump station. Fees run $17 for a tent site, $19 with hookups.

Little Talbot Island State Park—(904) 251–2320, western side of Little Talbot Island along Myrtle Creek, approximately a quarter mile from the beach. Forty campsites, each with water, electricity, an in-ground fire ring, and a picnic table. Rest rooms/showers, a dump station, small boat ramp, nature trail, playground. A primitive camping area is available for groups and organizations. Pets are allowed with current vaccination. Fees are $10 from October through February, $14 from March through September.

Huguenot Memorial Park—(904) 251–3335. No hookups; $7.88 for RVs, $5.63 for tents.

Hanna Park—(904) 249–4700. You'll find 293 sites with electric/water/sewer hookups on all, along with rest rooms/showers and a general store. It costs $18.00 for RVs, $13.50 for tents.

Other Points of Interest

Amelia Island Museum of History—(904) 261–7378, 233 South 3rd Street, Fernandina Beach, www.ameliaisland.com/museum. Located within the old Nassau County Jailhouse, this is the only oral history museum in Florida. Guides take you through an engaging 4,000 years of the island's history, and it's particular importance as a thriving port in nineteenth-century Florida. Walk-in tours at 11:00 A.M. and 2:00 P.M., Monday through Saturday.

Black Heritage Trail—(904) 798–9111. Trace northeastern Florida's black history through nine sites: American Beach, Catherine Street Fire Station, Kingsley Plantation, Masonic Temple, Mount Zion A.M.E. (African Methodist Episcopal) Church, Bethel Baptist Institutional Church, Edward Waters College, Olustee Battlefield, and Edwin Stanton School. Call the Jacksonville and the Beaches Convention and Visitors Bureau for a trail guide.

Cummer Museum of Art and Gardens—(904) 356–6857, 829 Riverside Avenue, Jacksonville. The permanent collection spans twelve galleries and features an impressive array of Western art from 2000 B.C. to the present. Open Tuesday through Friday 10:00 A.M.–4:00 P.M., Saturday noon–5:00 P.M., Sunday 2:00–5:00 P.M., $5.00.

Fort Caroline National Memorial—(904) 641–7155, 12713 Fort Caroline Road, Arlington. French Huguenots landed at this site in 1564, establishing the first Protestant colony in North America. It encompasses 680 acres and includes a replica of the fort, a museum filled with French and Native American artifacts, and a nature trail. Open daily 9:00 A.M.–5:00 P.M., free.

Jacksonville Maritime Museum—(904) 398–9011 at Southbank Riverwalk, (904) 355–9011 at Jacksonville Landing. Model ships, paintings, photos, and artifacts relating to local maritime history beginning in 1842 and continuing through World War II. Landing: Monday through Saturday 11:00 A.M.–7:00 P.M., Sunday 1:00–5:00 P.M.; Riverwalk: Monday through Saturday 11:00 A.M.–4:00 P.M., Sunday 1:00–5:00 P.M.; free.

Jacksonville Museum of Contemporary Art—(904) 398–8336, 4160 Boulevard Center Drive. The permanent collection includes art by Louise Nevelson, a variety of modern paintings, an impressive pre-Columbian art exhibit, and a sculpture garden. Open Tuesday, Wednesday, and Friday 10:00 A.M.–4:00 P.M., Thursday 10:00 A.M.–10:00 P.M., Saturday and Sunday 1:00–5:00 P.M.; $2.00–3.00.

Jacksonville Zoological Gardens—(904) 757–4463, 8605 Zoo Road. The *Birds of the Rift Valley Aviary* features more than seventy-five birds in free flight. A 1,200-foot boardwalk overlooks animals on the twenty-acre *Plains of East Africa* exhibit, and *Mahali Pa Simba* (place of the lions) is a one-acre home to two adult lions and two lion cubs. The *Okavango Village* features unique animals that can be viewed from a boardwalk along the Trout River, which leads to a domesticated animal petting area. Daily 9:00 A.M.–5:00 P.M.; $4.00–6.50.

Region 1

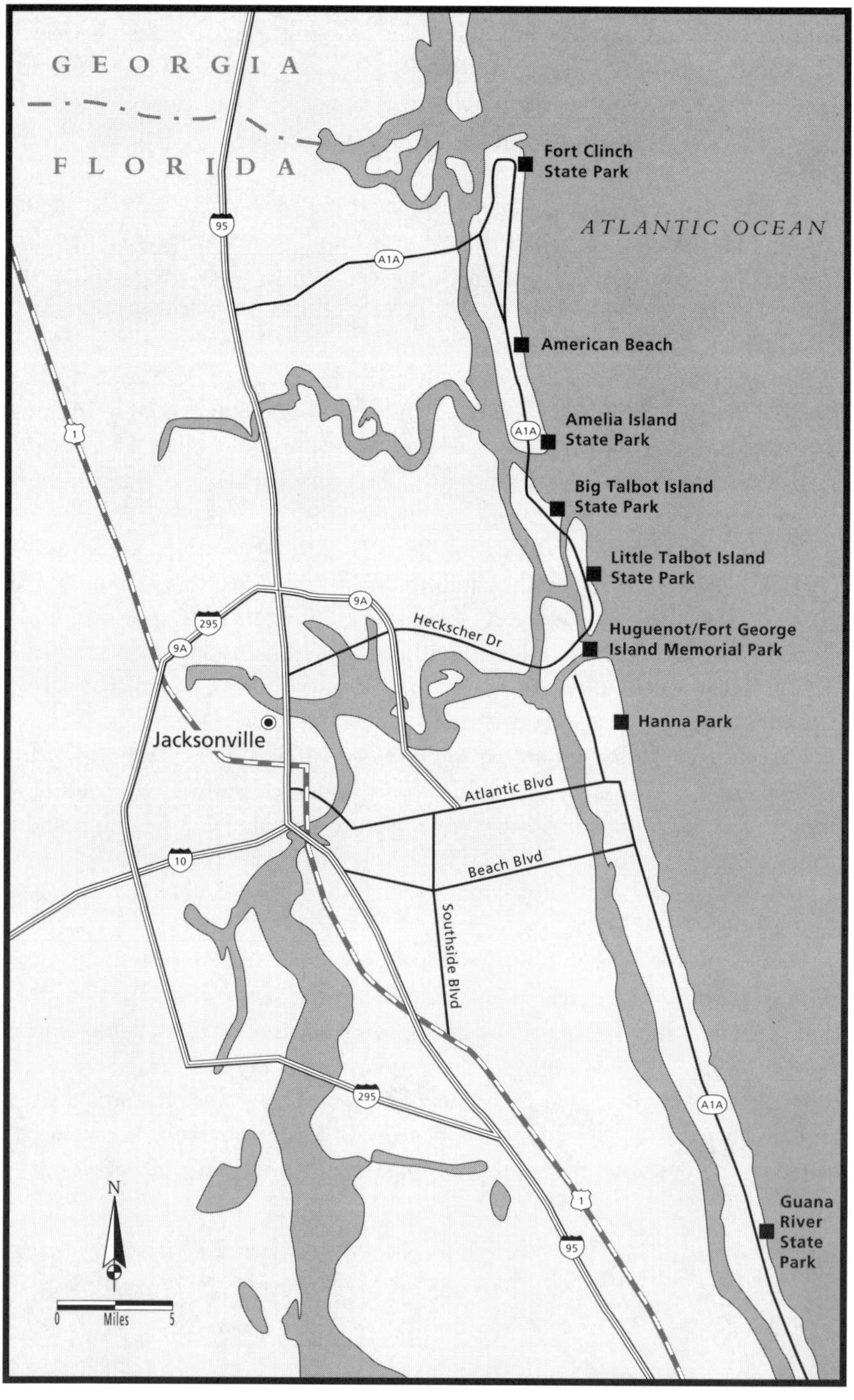

GEORGIA
FLORIDA
ATLANTIC OCEAN
95
A1A
1
Fort Clinch State Park
American Beach
Amelia Island State Park
Big Talbot Island State Park
Little Talbot Island State Park
Huguenot/Fort George Island Memorial Park
Hanna Park
Guana River State Park
9A
295
Heckscher Dr
Jacksonville
Atlantic Blvd
Beach Blvd
Southside Blvd
10
N
0 Miles 5

Fort Clinch State Park

With Georgia facing you across the mouth of the St. Mary's River, this is the farthest north you can go to the beach in Florida. On the east side of the park lies the open Atlantic and huge, windswept sand dunes. A fishing pier extends for a half mile out from the northeastern tip, and by the time you reach the end of it you feel like you're out in the middle of the ocean. The fishing potential is limitless here, given the abundance of sea life from the meeting of the St. Mary's and the Atlantic, along with the relative lack of fishermen using these waters. Sandy beach winds around from the ocean to the banks of the river, and you can stroll for ages. The waters near the jetty are pro-

Firing the cannons at Fort Clinch.

tected from wind and surf during fall and winter northeasters, though the water gets pretty chilly then for swimming. There are hiking trails through the lush, hardwood hammock, with alligators in some of the ponds. A 6-mile mountain bike trail through the hammock is one of the great attractions for area fat-tire enthusiasts. Because the hammock is made up of many uneven mounds, the twisting, narrow track is one of the more challenging bike rides you can find in Florida.

There are two campgrounds, one by the Amelia River and the other one out by the beach. Many of the tourists who come here are from Georgia, and the high season for some reason doesn't conform with any others in Florida. Spring is the busiest time here, when RVs fill most of the campsites. At other times of year, though, it's not that difficult to get a site. In October a full-garrison reenactment by Confederate soldiers takes place at the fort, with another one in May by Union soldiers.

Pentagonally shaped, the fort is located so that four of its five bastions look out toward the water. Strolling through dark tunnels and archways from room to room in the bastions, you find the place much bigger than you would imagine. Sunlight leaks into this gloom via riflemen's slits in the wall. Narrow, winding stairways take you up onto the ramparts, from which you can circumnavigate the fort. The views are panoramic from here, staring opposite at Cumberland Island National Seashore and out the mouth of the St. Mary's River.

ACCESS: From I–95, take exit 129 east onto A1A/200 for 14 miles to the town of Fernandina Beach; follow signs to the beach and park entrance.

PARKING: Large parking lots.

HOURS/FEES: 8:00 A.M.–sunset; $3.25 entrance fee per vehicle.

AMENITIES: Rest rooms, showers, picnic areas, mountain bike trails, dune walkovers, hiking trails, campground, fishing jetty, historic fort.

ACTIVITIES: Fort exploration, mountain biking, swimming, hiking, fishing, surfing, camping.

FOR MORE INFORMATION: Fort Clinch State Park (904) 277–7274.

American Beach

While the beach itself here may not be quite up to the incredible level of the state parks to the north at Fort Clinch and to the south at Little Talbot, this unique community is definitely worth a visit. In 1930, A. L. Lewis, president of the Afro-American Insurance Company in Jacksonville, bought 200 acres of land on Amelia Island to provide a safe beach environment for his employees to enjoy. This purchase was one of the inspirations for Mary McLeod Bethune and friends to do something similar down in New Smyrna Beach. For almost seventy-five years, it has been one of the favorite beaches for black residents of Jacksonville to congregate and socialize at; from 1930 to 1970 it was run as a resort that blacks came to from all over the country. Under pressure from development, now squashed between the Amelia Island Plantation and the Ritz-Carlton, the community has dwindled to only about one hundred acres. Still, it has fought valiantly to survive, and residents have applied to get their old homes restored in conjunction with the National Register of Historic Places.

MaVynne Betsch, the great-granddaughter of A. L. Lewis, is the most visible figure behind the fight to save American Beach. A striking 6 feet tall, with a mass of wavy dreadlocks, the sixty-five-year-old Betsch attended Oberlin College and sang opera in Europe when she was young. She runs a museum out of her trailer, educating visitors in the local history and black history of the area. An excellent book by Jacksonville native Marsha Dean Phelts, *An American Beach for African Americans*, tells the story of the place in loving detail. Phelts remembers her visits to the resort in the 1950s as being like going to Disney World. A PBS documentary also captured the history, and the community has been the subject of articles in numerous national papers. Still, not much of the media attention has translated into money to ensure the town's survival, so Betsch keeps a constant vigil. Communities like American Beach are as much a symbol of old Florida as the state parks are, and a visit here will give you a perspective on Florida history that you'll find few other places.

ACCESS: From I–95, take exit 129 east to Amelia Island/Fernandina Beach. Drive 11 miles on A1A to Amelia Island Parkway. After a mile the parkway becomes CR105A; stay on CR105A for 4 miles to Lewis Street, turn left, and go to the end.

PARKING: Street parking.

HOURS/FEES: Twenty-four hours; free.

AMENITIES: American Beach trailer museum.

ACTIVITIES: Sunbathing, swimming, black history.

FOR MORE INFORMATION: American Beach (904) 261–3248.

Amelia Island State Park

On the north side of Nassau Sound, this spot is yet another in the glut of fine state park beaches north of Jacksonville. Taking up 200 acres, it changes from beach to coastal forest to salt marsh as you come around the outside edge of the sound and head under the bridge. The bridge is open to fishermen along its mile long-length; relatively low to the water, it's a good place to fish from. And would you believe this is one of the only state parks in Florida where you can ride sea horses! Well, not really. But you can ride horses by the sea, rented from the Kelly Seahorse Ranch at the park. At the opposite end of Amelia Island from Fort Clinch, this is one of the only other wilderness beaches on the island available to the public.

ACCESS: From the north on I–95, take exit 129 east to Amelia Island/ Fernandina Beach on A1A and follow signs for A1A south. The entrance is 8 miles south of Fernandina Beach just before you cross the bridge over Nassau Sound.

From the south on I–95, exit east at exit 124A (Heckscher Drive). Follow this 22 miles as it turns into A1A north 7 miles past Little Talbot State Park.

PARKING: Parking lot.

HOURS/FEES: 8:00 A.M.–sunset; $1.00 entrance fee.

AMENITIES: Rest rooms, horse stables, fishing bridge.

ACTIVITIES: Horseback riding, sunbathing, swimming, birding, fishing, hiking.

FOR MORE INFORMATION: Amelia Island State Park (904) 251–2320. Kelly Seahorse Ranch (904) 261–4878.

Big Talbot Island State Park

While Big Talbot Island is larger in size than its little sister, it has far less Atlantic beach frontage. Most of the beach, in fact, borders on the wild waters of Nassau Sound, the last remaining natural inlet in Florida. But we're talking apples and oranges here. You don't go to Big Talbot for a typical beach experience. What Big Talbot Island provides is a tribute to erosion—the magnificent power of wind and waves in sculpting a coastline.

The dead trees that line the beach of Big Talbot are a photographer's dream. All sizes and shapes of gnarled root structures stand like ghostly sen-

The dead trees on Big Talbot Island are a photographer's dream.

tinels along the miles of beach outside the Nassau Sound bridge. Forests of southern magnolia and live oak are constantly battered by erosion, and the high bluffs keep receding to sacrifice more trees to the eclectic collection of ghosts. Driftwood also rolls in and joins the array. A hiking path, Blackrock Trail, wanders through the coastal forest along the bluffs.

A boat ramp on the west side of the park gives the options of river or ocean access, though it's wise to only venture out into the Atlantic on calm days. Like Little Talbot, the fishing is excellent here, and fly fishing for redfish is becoming more and more popular in the creeks. "Tailing reds" can be spotted with their fins out of the water during the spring and fall flood tides.

It's not a good swimming beach because of all the roots, but it's a great walking beach. The intrepid adventurer with a small kayak can paddle out to a nearby sand island in the middle of Nassau Sound. With nothing but seagulls for company, it's a magical piece of seclusion.

ACCESS: From the north on I–95, take exit 129 east to Amelia Island/Fernandina Beach on A1A, then follow signs for A1A south. The entrance is on your left 10 miles south of Fernandina Beach shortly after you cross the bridge over Nassau Sound.

From the south on I–95, exit east at exit 124A (Heckscher Drive). Follow this 22 miles as it turns into A1A north, past Little Talbot State Park, to the park entrance on your right.

PARKING: Beachside parking lot.

HOURS/FEES: 8:00 A.M.–sunset; self-pay $2.00 entrance fee per vehicle.

AMENITIES: Rest rooms.

ACTIVITIES: Sunbathing, photography, canoeing, hiking.

FOR MORE INFORMATION: Big Talbot Island State Park (904) 251–2320.

Little Talbot Island State Park

Part of the Talbot Islands GeoPark, the 5 miles of lovely beaches at Little Talbot are some of the most wonderfully undisturbed ones in North Florida. This is the place for a latter-day Robinson Crusoe, with wide stretches of sand to walk the day away upon. Huge rolling dunes lie between the coastal forests and the beach, and on the west side of the island are salt marshes. The park encompasses the whole island of Little Talbot, offering a lot of recreational possibilities. You can rent canoes to paddle through the marshes, bicycles to circumnavigate the island, and horseshoes and volleyball equipment to have a sporting game. The surf fishing is great, and the river fishing is pretty good, too. This is around the southern limits for striped bass, or "stripers." Migrating shorebirds give the bird-watcher plenty to look out for during the off-season months; you can pick up a brochure listing 194 different species that the island hosts at the ranger station. The 4-mile hiking trail takes you through a diversity of ecosystems, and the magnolia forests are quite beautiful. There is both a regular campground and a youth group camping area.

This is a place to truly stretch out and wiggle your toes in the sand to your heart's delight. The beaches north of Jacksonville have been traditionally overlooked by everyone except vacationing Georgians, but they are one of the great treasures of Florida. Now that Jacksonville is finally achieving its dream of becoming a destination city in Florida, more people are beginning to discover them.

ACCESS: From I–95, exit east at exit 124A (Heckscher Drive). Follow this 17 miles to the park entrance.

From the south on A1A, take the Mayport Ferry across the St. Johns River; go 5 miles north on A1A. The park will be on your right.

From the north on A1A, the park is 14 miles south of Fernandina Beach.

PARKING: Beachside parking lots.

HOURS/FEES: 8:00 A.M.–sunset; $3.25 entrance fee per vehicle, $1.00 walk-in or ride-in.

AMENITIES: Rest rooms, showers, pavilions, dune walkovers, hiking trail, campground, canoe, bike, volleyball, and horseshoe rentals.

ACTIVITIES: Swimming, volleyball, horseshoes, canoeing, bicycling, hiking, fishing, surfing, camping.

FOR MORE INFORMATION: Little Talbot Island State Park (904) 251–2320.

Huguenot Memorial Park/Fort George Island

Huguenot Memorial Park, on the north side of the St. Johns River, is the northern twin of the city of Jacksonville's two fantastic beach parks. Sometimes overlooked because it's being slightly harder to access than the main beaches to the south, the park is still very popular in summertime. It's a 450-acre peninsula, surrounded by the Fort George Inlet to the north, the St. Johns River on its southern flank, and the Atlantic Ocean on the eastern side. As you cruise in from the park entrance, the St. Johns is on your right, and you can drive your car out on the beach along the river. In fact, you can drive your car on the beaches all around the park, except for one marked 500-foot section.

Waterfront camping without hookups is allowed in different areas of the park, and the rates are surprisingly cheap. During the summer, plenty of Jax locals take advantage of these rates to barbecue, splash, and fish the weekend away. The dunes and sea oats are in the state that wild beaches should be, and the raw natural beauty of the park is an interesting contrast to the major shipping lane that passes by it and the Mayport Naval Station across the river. Swimming is great in almost any of the park's waters, and sailboarders are particularly attracted to the Fort George Inlet lagoon. The water is fairly shallow throughout it, and it can hold high winds without getting very rough.

The Atlantic-side beach is a wonderful, wide expanse, with the long north jetty of the St. Johns River bordering the southern end. This jetty is a fishing hot spot, because it extends far out into the ocean and allows fishing access to the fertile zone where Florida's largest river meets the sea. Bait concessions are open during the summer, along with food concessions for hungry beachgoers. Safety is provided in the park by two JSO (Jacksonville Sheriff's Office) police officers stationed there full time. With the nominal entry fee and endless possibilities for recreation, this is perhaps the finest beach owned by a major city in all of Florida.

ACCESS: From the north on I–95, exit on SR 9A east and continue 7 miles to SR 105 (Heckscher Drive); turn left and go east for 11 miles to Fort George Inlet. Look for the park entrance on your right 1.5 miles past the Mayport Ferry.

From the south on I–95, after crossing the second bridge in Jacksonville (over the Trout River), exit east onto SR 105 (Heckscher Drive). Follow this 19 miles to Fort George Inlet; look for park entrance on your right 1.5 miles past the Mayport Ferry.

From the south on A1A, take the Mayport Ferry across the St. Johns River and go 1.5 miles north on A1A. The park will be on your right.

From the north on A1A, it's 20 miles south of Fernandina Beach.

PARKING: Free parking lots.

HOURS/FEES: 8:00 A.M.–sunset; 50-cent entrance fee.

You can drive on the beaches in Huguenot Memorial Park.

AMENITIES: Rest rooms, showers, campground, summer lifeguards, summer concessions.

ACTIVITIES: Sunbathing, swimming, hiking, fishing, surfing, camping, sailboarding, beach driving.

FOR MORE INFORMATION: Huguenot Memorial Park (904) 251–3335.

Hanna Park

After the relatively glum beaches around Jacksonville Beach, the huge city park at the north end of the Jax beaches is a wonderful surprise. Hanna Park is everything an urban beach park should be—and then some. Covering 450 acres and 1.5 miles of beachfront, the park encompasses a wide beach, healthy dunes, a freshwater lake, woods, trails, campsites, and a general store. There's little development anywhere around, and it's hard to believe this place is so close to a major city.

The beach is beautiful, brilliant white sand giving way to a tan color near the water. Surfing, sailboarding, fishing, and swimming are all good things to enjoy, and the beach has lifeguards in summer. That's definitely the busiest time here, when much of Jacksonville comes out to enjoy the park. There is an enormous campground spread out through the woods, with almost 300 campsites. They all have electric, water, and sewer hookups, and are favored by large numbers of RV travelers from Georgia at certain times of year.

Interestingly enough, what Hanna Park is most famous for is mountain biking. Off-road bikers from all over the northern part of Florida come here to ride, due to the extensive and well-maintained trail system. One of the fixtures at the park and a man responsible for a lot of the trail building and upkeep is a character named Bunky Cross. He started doing the work on his own, maintaining old trails and eventually creating new extra-challenging ones, and park supervisors wholeheartedly approved of his work. In fact, they liked him so much they started letting him in for free. He takes care to leave virtually all trees intact when making his trails, and everybody knows from the tight, twisting turns when they're on a Bunky trail.

The sixty-acre freshwater lake in the park is used for swimming and fishing, and is a good alternative to the Atlantic when the ocean's a bit rough. There's even a special children's play area of the lake with fountains and squirters.

ACCESS: From the north on I–95, take the Jacksonville Beaches exit from downtown Jacksonville and get onto Atlantic Boulevard; go 10 miles. Take the Mayport Road exit (toward the Mayport base—north) and follow the road for 5 miles until you're close to the end. You will see signs for Kathryn Abbey Hanna Park. Turn right off Mayport onto Wonderwood Drive into the park.

From the south on I–95, exit onto SR 115 (Southside Boulevard) and go north for 10 miles to Atlantic Boulevard east; go 7 miles on Atlantic, take the Mayport Road exit (toward the Mayport base—north), and follow the road for 5 miles until you're close to the end. You will see signs for Kathryn Abbey Hanna Park. Turn right off Mayport onto Wonderwood Drive into the park.

PARKING: Huge parking lots.

HOURS/FEES: 8:00 A.M.–sunset; $1.00 entrance fee.

AMENITIES: Mountain bike trails, rest rooms, showers, freshwater lake, general store, campground, summer lifeguards, summer food concessions.

ACTIVITIES: Biking, sunbathing, swimming, hiking, fishing, surfing, camping, sailboarding.

FOR MORE INFORMATION: Hanna Park (904) 249–4700.

Guana River State Park

Though state parks in Florida are designed to preserve "old Florida," most do so with an abundance of amenities and interpretive programs. Guana River, which was bought by the state in 1984, takes a different approach. Here the emphasis is all on nature. The only facilities you'll find are rest rooms and an observation tower, because the tract was purchased in such an undeveloped state that they decided to leave it just as it was.

The beach is just over 4 miles long, and is notable for being one of the only public beach accesses between St. Augustine and Jacksonville. There are two main areas, North Beach and South Beach. The access is from the west side of A1A, because all the parking and the bulk of the park is located on that side of the road. You have to walk across A1A from the parking areas, and you need to keep an eye out for speeding traffic. At North Beach, an observation tower sits on one of the highest sand dunes in Florida, 40 feet

above sea level, offering sweeping views of the surrounding ocean and the tidal marshes of the Tolomato and Guana Rivers.

On the river side, 9 miles of nature trails and old service roads run through the woods and grasslands of the park. If you've got a mountain bike or beach cruiser, these trails are a lot of fun to ride. It's a great place to go birding, and peregrine falcons visit in early October. The park offers a guided nature walk on one Saturday a month from September through May, which begins at eight in the morning. After the two-hour walk, coffee, orange juice, doughnuts, and muffins are served. The cost is only $5.00, which is worth it just for breakfast! Fishing is popular both on the beach and at the dammed-up freshwater area known as Guana Lake. This area was dammed in 1957 to flood the upwater marshes, with the intent of creating a hunting preserve for waterfowl. Alligators and otters inhabit the freshwater zones, and blue crabs and large shrimp favor the brackish areas near the dam.

ACCESS: From I–95, exit onto SR 16 (exit 94) east to St. Augustine, turn right onto San Marcos Avenue, go 0.5 mile to May Street, turn left, and follow signs to Vilano Beach and A1A north. Follow A1A for 8 miles to the park entrance on your left.

On A1A, the park is 9 miles south of Jacksonville Beach.

PARKING: Parking lots.

HOURS/FEES: 8:00 A.M.–sunset; $2.00 entrance fee.

AMENITIES: Rest rooms, observation tower, dune crossovers, unlimited nature.

ACTIVITIES: Canoeing, sunbathing, swimming, hiking, fishing.

FOR MORE INFORMATION: Guana River State Park (904) 825–5071.

Opposite page: Guana River State Park.

The Town of Eight Flags

Old Fernandina, the original Spanish settlement on Amelia Island that dates back to the eighteenth century, was a hotly contested piece of real estate. Known as the "Town of Eight Flags," it was not only subject to the French, British, and Spanish machinations over Florida but also claimed by some rather unlikely countries for brief periods. In 1812 a group of American settlers proclaimed a republic there, but were unwilling to challenge Spanish control of St. Augustine. A Scottish soldier of fortune, Gregor McGregor, captured Fernandina in 1817, and resisted attacks by both Spanish and volunteer American forces. His claim there was soon succeeded by that of Luis Aury, a pirate of Mexican heritage. Aury claimed Amelia Island for Mexico and flew a homemade Mexican flag over it, since Mexico didn't have a national flag at the time.

Due to its convenient location for smuggling, Fernandina gained notoriety as a riotous town of smugglers, pirates, and general outlaws of all sorts until Florida became part of the United States in 1821. There's not much left of the original settlement, but the newer "old town" Fernandina has been lovingly restored. This area was built up in the mid-1800s around the time Fort Clinch was built. Nineteenth-century houses with beautiful gardens line the main street, some of them converted to homey bed-and-breakfasts. At the Amelia Island Museum a few blocks away, the only way of seeing much of the collection is through a unique oral history tour that takes you through the island's extraordinary past.

Fort Clinch was meant to protect the port of Fernandina, along with coastal and interior shipping. Work on the fort progressed at a crawl, and it was less than half finished when the Confederacy captured it without resistance in 1861. They held it for no more than a year, though, before General Robert E. Lee called for its evacuation. Union troops had already captured coastal islands in South Carolina and Georgia, and their gunboats forced a hasty retreat from Fort Clinch.

By the time the fort was finally finished, masonry forts were obsolete due to the increased firepower of rifled cannons. Shortly after completion it was deactivated. It was only used again briefly in the Spanish-American War and during World War II as a coastal lookout station. The Civil War reenactments here are impressive, especially the firing of the cannons. A haze of gunpowder smoke surrounds the soldiers and tourists after each almighty thunderclap. Having conversations with the soldiers is a little strange, since they stay faithfully in their time period. A captain told two female visitors who said they were nurses that he could hardly believe that possible, nursing being a male job. He also noted that their indecent attire—shorts—made it unlikely that any officer would ever consider them for marriage material.

Region 2

The trail through historic Florida takes a turn way back in time when you enter the town of St. Augustine, the first Spanish settlement in Florida. Fort Castillo de San Marcos is a spectacular attraction and well worth stopping by for a visit. The visitor information center next door at 10 Castillo Drive is a good place to leave your vehicle and set out from. Cruising out of the tourist bustle of town to the barrier island and A1A, things quiet down again. Anastasia State Park is a great beach that encompasses a whole peninsula, with some of North Florida's best surf. Frank Butler Park is a nice county facility near Crescent Beach, and at the bottom of Anastasia Island is another historic attraction in Fort Matanzas. Beach driving is allowed through most of St. Johns County from approved access points.

Just south of Marineland in Flagler County is Washington Oaks State Gardens, a beautiful set of gardens with a beach known to most as The Rocks. It's one of the only appearances of coquina rock on the surface in the north of the state. At the bottom end of the county is Gamble Rogers State Recreation Area, which has camping.

The sands of Ormond Beach were the site of some of the earliest auto racing, with automotive pioneers Ransom Olds and Alexander Winton running turn-of-the-twentieth-century automobiles neck and neck at 57 miles per hour down the beach. That's a pretty exciting speed to drive on a beach today—and highly illegal with 10 mph speed limits—but imagine in 1903! The two-cylinder Olds car was known as "The Pirate," and the Winton car was "The Bullet." In recent years a replica of The Pirate was made to be shown off at local celebrations, and the retirement of the Oldsmobile brand was a great blow to the area's long association with Ransom Olds. These days Ormond is a very quiet neighbor to Daytona Beach, and the Oceanfront and Bicentennial county parks are rarely crowded. For even more peace, the North Peninsula State Park is an untouched stretch without facilities.

For some it's Shangri-la, and for others it's Hades, but there's definitely no other place quite like Daytona Beach in the state of Florida. While Daytona

Beach proper encapsulates about a 5-mile stretch of beach, the greater area that is often referred to as Daytona includes more than 20 miles of beaches. Fine-grained sand results in a dense, hardpack surface that automobiles can drive on, and beach driving has been part of Daytona's history for almost a century.

Because of the beach driving, Daytona Beach has long been a natural magnet for college students on spring break, and even more so after Fort Lauderdale declared them persona non grata. Even Daytona's notorious tolerance for wild partying met its limit when the additional crush surged into town, though. They kept open arms out, but did less to encourage students to come, eventually bringing the crowds back down to the same manageable level they had been. Part of the reason for this has been the huge success of Bike Week in Daytona Beach, and the desire to devote more resources to attracting motorcycle enthusiasts. Close to a half million people showed up in 2001 for the annual motorcycle extravaganza in the first week of March—and bikers spend a lot more money than college students do. Only ten to fifteen years ago, Bike Week was more the exclusive domain of Harley Davidson riders and hard-core bikers, and hardly the kind of scene a resort community would wish to promote. Now it brings in every kind of motorcycle rider imaginable, and though it's still not quite what you'd call a family atmosphere, a fun time is definitely had by all.

Meandering out of the commercialism of Daytona, the dead end down at Ponce Inlet is Lighthouse County Park, a sedate place with good surfing and fishing, as well as an old lighthouse to visit.

Access

From the north, take exit 95 east from I–95 to US 1, turn right into St. Augustine, and follow signs to A1A south.

From the south, take exit 85 east from I–95 at Port Orange to the beaches and A1A.

Beaches

Anastasia State Park
Frank Butler Park
Fort Matanzas National Monument
Washington Oaks State Gardens aka The Rocks
Gamble Rogers Memorial State Recreation Area at Flagler Beach
Oceanfront Park
Bicentennial Park

Daytona Beach
Lighthouse Point Park

Camping

Anastasia State Park—(904) 461–2033. There are 139 sites here with picnic table, in-ground grill, fire ring and water; 104 with electricity; a dump station is available. Reservations up to eleven months in advance. October through January, $14; February through September, $16. Electricity costs $2.00, an extra car $3.00, pets $2.00 per night each.

Gamble Rogers Memorial State Recreation Area—(904) 517–2086. Thirty-four beachfront sites, all with electric (thirty amp), water, picnic tables, and ground grills. Rest rooms, hot showers, RV dump station. Very busy in February and March. Fees run $20.67 a day with electric, $18.53 a day without electric, tax included.

Spruce Creek Park—(904) 736–5953, 6250 South Ridgewood Avenue, Port Orange.

The park has a fishing pier, hiking trail, tent camping, and a picnic area.

Other Points of Interest

Castillo de San Marcos—(904) 829–6506, 1 Castillo Drive in downtown St. Augustine. The first fort built by the Spanish in 1695, it literally sucked up cannonballs and remains the well-preserved centerpiece of the town. Admission costs $4.00.

St. Augustine Lighthouse—(904) 829–0745, 81 Lighthouse Avenue, St. Augustine. Gorgeous view of the town; 219 steps. The site includes a museum of lighthouse artifacts and lore. Admission is $4.00.

Marineland—(904) 471–1111, 9507 Oceanshore Boulevard, Marineland. The venerable seaquarium has fallen on hard times with the competition in Orlando, but it's still home to a lot of wonderful creatures. The fee is $14.95 for adults, $9.95 for those under twelve.

Flagler Beach Pier—(904) 439–4169, 215 South A1A, Flagler Beach.

Tomoka State Park—(904) 676–4050, 3 miles north of Ormond Beach. A park of massive oaks near the confluence of the Tomoka and Halifax Rivers. Great hiking and boating. Admission costs $3.25.

The Casements Cultural Center—(904) 676–3216, 25 Riverside Drive, Ormond Beach. John D. Rockefeller's old winter home, restored to beautiful condition and home to a collection of Hungarian art.

Museum of Arts and Sciences—(904) 255–0285, 1040 Museum Boulevard, Daytona Beach.

Region 2

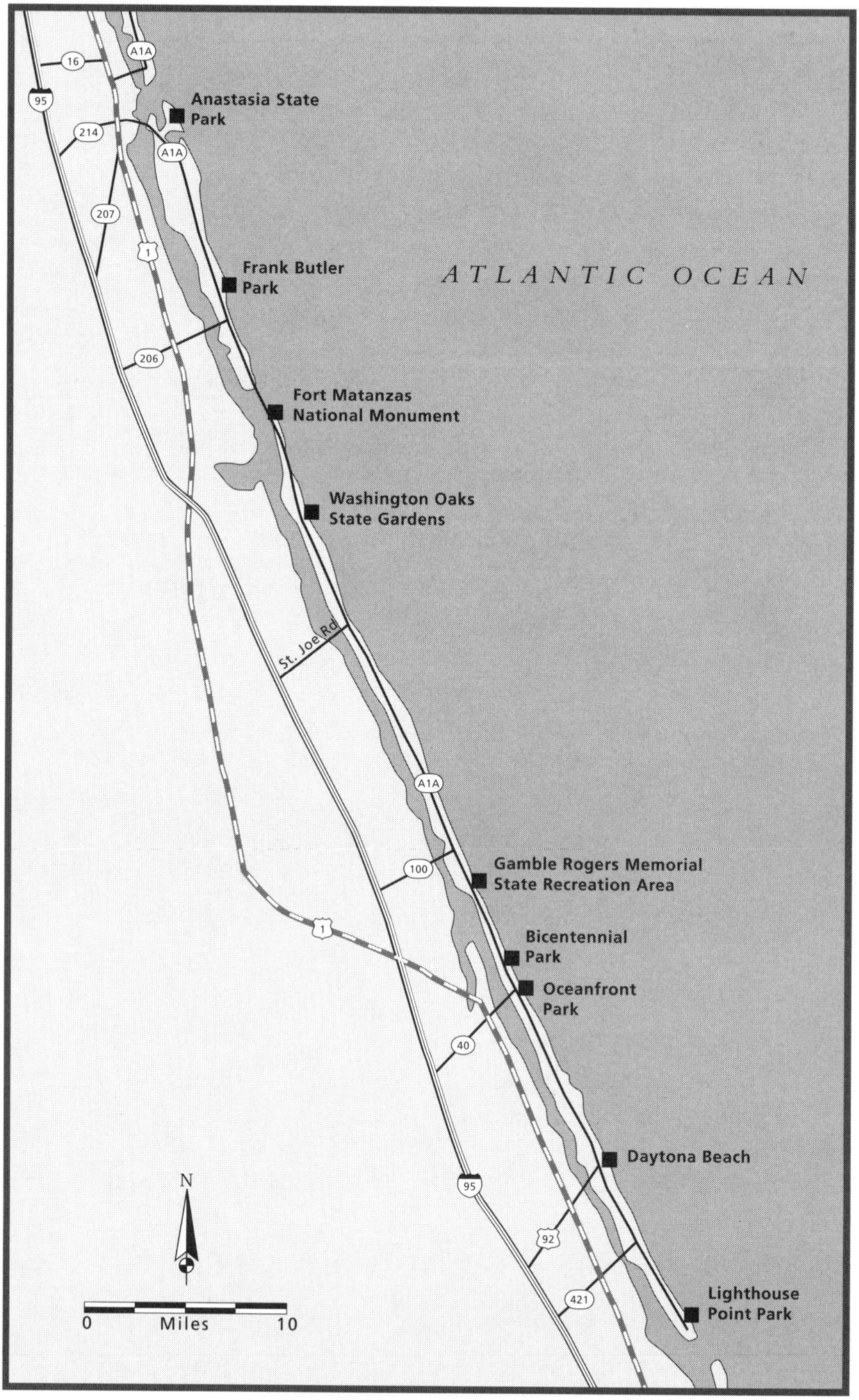

16
A1A
95
Anastasia State Park
214
A1A
207
1
Frank Butler Park
ATLANTIC OCEAN
206
Fort Matanzas National Monument
Washington Oaks State Gardens
St. Joe Rd
A1A
100
Gamble Rogers Memorial State Recreation Area
1
Bicentennial Park
Oceanfront Park
40
Daytona Beach
N
95
92
421
Lighthouse Point Park
0
Miles
10

Anastasia State Park

Anastasia Island is one of the most beautiful coastal parks on the northeast coast of Florida, and it's just a short distance from all the colonial history of Florida's oldest city, St. Augustine. Though it's really a peninsula rather than an island, Anastasia seems disconnected from modern times. The island is made up mostly of beach, sand dunes, tidal marsh, and coastal hammock. Beautiful white sand, wide beaches, and miles of room to spread out make it an enviable place to spend time. Beach driving is allowed north of the access ramp all the way up to the inlet. Until the summer of 2000, you were able to drive in on the beach from the south, which local surfers took advantage of to avoid buying park passes. That is no longer allowed, and the only access to driving on the beach is from within the park. Close to the inlet is one of the best surf breaks in North Florida, a spot called Blowhole.

In Salt Run Lagoon on the west side of the park, sailboards are available for rent along with lessons, and a special area is set aside for sailboarding. Fishing is good in the lagoon and also up past the bird-nesting area by the jetties. Hiking can be enjoyed along the nature trail through the hammock, amid shady surroundings of ancient oaks and Spanish moss.

The campsites here are some of the best to be found at any Florida beach park. They're located back from the beach in the shade of the oak hammock—thus they're free from blowing sand and sun, but just a short walk from the beach.

ACCESS: From the north on I–95, take exit 94 onto SR 214 east to St. Augustine. Cross the Bridge of Lions and follow Anastasia Boulevard 1.5 miles south to the park entrance.

From the south on I–95, take exit 93 onto SR 207 east to St. Augustine. After 4 miles turn right onto SR 312 and follow it across the river to the park entrance.

On A1A, the park is 1.5 miles south of St. Augustine.

PARKING: Free parking lots.

HOURS/FEES: 8:00 A.M.–sunset; $3.25 entrance fee.

AMENITIES: Showers, rest rooms, summer lifeguards, sailboard and canoe rentals, picnic areas, campsite.

ACTIVITIES: Camping, surfing, sailboarding, canoeing, swimming, sunbathing, hiking, fishing, beach driving, picnicking.

FOR MORE INFORMATION: Anastasia State Park (904) 461–2033.

Frank Butler Park

This county facility covers both sides of A1A from the ocean to the river, just north of the town of Crescent Beach. There's a boat ramp on the west side into the Matanzas River, and it's a popular launching spot for area boaters. Both sides of the road have rest rooms, so it's not necessary to make a mad dash across A1A should nature call. Shady pavilions overlook the water and make for nice luncheon spots. There are nearby access points for beach driving, but the beach is closed to traffic at night during the summer months for turtle nesting. The beach is a little better for driving up here than it is down by Matanzas and there's usually a nice wide strand—unlike the badly eroded area around St. Augustine Pier a few miles to the north.

Offshore sandbars knock down the waves a lot, but it's still prudent to take care while swimming. St. Johns County doesn't have a year-round lifeguard crew, and the beaches are patrolled only during summer.

Frank Butler Park.

ACCESS: From I–95, take exit 92 onto SR 206 east to Crescent Beach. Turn left onto A1A and go 1 mile north.

On A1A, the park is 5 miles north of Matanzas Inlet, 10 miles south of St. Augustine.

PARKING: Free parking lot

HOURS/FEES: Twenty-four hours; free. Beach driving costs $3.00 a day, $20.00 annually. It's available twenty-four hours October through April; 5:00 A.M.–10:00 P.M. from May through September.

AMENITIES: Boat ramp, showers, rest rooms, summer lifeguards, picnic tables.

ACTIVITIES: Sunbathing, boating, swimming, surfing, picnicking.

FOR MORE INFORMATION: St. Johns Parks and Recreation (904) 471–6616.

Fort Matanzas National Monument

At Matanzas Inlet, known ominously in history as "Bloody Matanzas," a small sister fort to Castillo de San Marcos acted as a sentinel to protect St. Augustine from southern intruders. The Spanish began their drive to colonize Florida with a massacre of French soldiers here in 1565. The massacre, or "matanza," gave name to the inlet, after a fleet of French Huguenots sailed to battle with the Spanish at St. Augustine and were instead shipwrecked to the south. When the Spanish found them, they ordered them to surrender and accept Catholicism. The French would do the former but not the latter, and 250 of them were massacred on the spot. In 1742 the Spanish built Fort Matanzas as they dug in to fend off the British. The masonry tower gave advanced warning of any ships sailing up from the south, and the cannon could blast any fleet that tried to sneak up the Matanzas River and attack from the backdoor.

The beach is easily accessible from the parking area, with good fishing, and occasionally spectacular surfing when the sandbars in the inlet have formed just right. On the river side, a half-mile boardwalk winds through coastal forest. The fort is located on Rattlesnake Island in the Matanzas River, and a free ferry offers tours of the fort every day. Historical reenactments take place periodically, with schedules on the park Web site, though at this time cannon firings are no longer occurring at Fort Matanzas.

Fort Matanzas.

ACCESS: From I–95, take exit 92 onto SR 206 east and go 6 miles to Crescent Beach; turn right on A1A, go 4 miles south to the park entrance.

On A1A, 15 miles south of St. Augustine.

PARKING: Free parking lot.

HOURS/FEES: 8:30 A.M.–5:30 P.M. every day except Christmas, free; tours of the fort are every hour from 9:30 A.M.–4:30 P.M.

AMENITIES: Boardwalk, visitor center, grills, rest rooms, showers, ferry to Rattlesnake Island, picnic tables.

ACTIVITIES: Historical tours, swimming, surfing, fishing, sunbathing, hiking.

FOR MORE INFORMATION:

Fort Matanzas National Monument (904) 471–0116.

Washington Oaks State Gardens aka The Rocks

Though you see the change start to happen with the grainier and softer sand in beaches of northern Volusia County, when you reach the beach known as The Rocks in Flagler County you learn the reason for it. Coquina rock, the underlying stratum that gives rise to such fantastic formations at Blowing Rocks in Jupiter and The Rocks in Stuart, comes to the surface again. The orange hues of the sand in this area, as opposed to the white-powder sands of Daytona, are a sure giveaway that coquina is close at hand. The beach is littered with scenic rock formations in all shapes and sizes, with tidal pools full of creatures such as anemones, starfish, and crabs.

A wooden boardwalk leads across the dunes to the beach, and the shoreline part of the 400-acre park extends for about a half mile. The fishing is good in the surf for bluefish, pompano, and whiting; on the Matanzas River side of the park, redfish, flounder, and sea trout can be expected. The gardens on the west side of A1A are, of course, the main attraction of this beautiful place. Set among towering live oaks that drip Spanish moss from their limbs, the gardens feature a combination of native and exotic plant life. The rose garden features many azaleas, camellias, and (of course) roses, with such names as Sweet Surrender, Don Juan, Kentucky Derby, and Cherokee Rose.

A number of hiking and biking trails are available. The Bella Vista trail system consists of a 1.7-mile loop through coastal hammock; a 0.5-mile hiking trail called the Mala Compra goes from the forest along the edge of the tidal marsh. You might need a vigorous walk or ride to revive you from the languor the gardens induce. Near the hiking trails are picnic facilities, rest rooms, and a children's play area. Ranger-led tours take place every Saturday and Sunday at 1:30 P.M., and they vary from beach walks to Florida Trail hikes to trips through the formal garden. Call the park to find out what the tours are for any given weekend.

The park is the site of the old Bella Vista plantation, started by General Joseph Hernandez, who led troops against the Seminole during the Second Seminole War. His daughter married a surveyor named George Washington, a relative of the first president. The place came to be renamed Washington Oaks by a couple who bought it in the 1930s.

ACCESS: From I–95, exit onto St. Joe Road east to Palm Coast, cross the 75-cent toll bridge to A1A, and go 5 miles north.

The Rocks at Washington Oaks State Gardens.

On A1A, the park is 2 miles south of Marineland, 10 miles north of Flagler Beach.

PARKING: Free parking lot.

HOURS/FEES: 8:00 A.M.–sunset; $3.25 entrance fee.

AMENITIES: Hiking and biking trails, gardens, showers, picnic tables, pavilion, rest rooms.

ACTIVITIES: Garden tours, sunbathing, swimming, surfing, fishing, picnicking, hiking, biking.

FOR MORE INFORMATION: Washington Oaks State Gardens (386) 446–6780.

Gamble Rogers Memorial State Recreation Area at Flagler Beach

This is a pretty river-to-ocean state park on a quiet stretch of coast. It has all the old Florida ambience that makes almost every state park a joy to visit, and best of all it has camping, which is a little more of a rarity in coastal parks. The thirty-four campsites in the park look out over the Atlantic, so you can enjoy the morning sunrise. On the west side of A1A bordering the river is the bulk of the 144-acre park, and during the evening beautiful sunsets take place. February and March are the peak times for visitors; it's hard to get a campsite without a reservation well in advance. Birds foraging around the tidal flats account for most of the wildlife, while turtles nest in abundance on the beach from May through September.

The beach is gently sloped, and offshore sandbars break down the waves. Bathing near shore is usually fairly safe, though the lack of lifeguards means that extra caution is warranted.

ACCESS: From the north on I–95, exit onto SR 100 east to Flagler Beach, turn right onto A1A, and go 3 miles south.

From the south on I–95, exit onto Old Dixie Highway east to A1A, turn left, and go 3 miles north.

From Daytona Beach, the park is 18 miles north on A1A.

PARKING: Free parking lot.

HOURS/FEES: 8:00 A.M.–sunset; $3.25 entrance fee riverside, $2.00 beachside.

AMENITIES: Showers, picnic tables, pavilion, rest rooms, campground, boat ramp, fishing dock, nature trail.

ACTIVITIES: Picnicking, sunbathing, swimming, surfing, fishing, camping.

FOR MORE INFORMATION: Gamble Rogers Memorial State Recreation Area at Flagler Beach (386) 517–2086.

Oceanfront Park

The Ormond Beach area is rich in history and has maintained a low-density, relaxed quality despite being adjacent to the bustle of Daytona Beach. After the railroad came through, Henry Flagler bought up the Halifax & St. Johns Railroad to incorporate into his FEC (Florida East Coast) line, and bought the Ormond Hotel as well. The community became a winter home for many industrial magnates, including John D. Rockefeller, who built a home known as "The Casements." It still stands today, and together with the Memorial Art Center and Gardens serves as the main historical and cultural attraction of the area.

There are two beautiful beaches in Ormond Beach. The first is Oceanfront Park, where the main east–west road through town comes to an end at the beach. There's a boardwalk, a full set of facilities, and as nice a beach as you could ask for. The beach at Ormond is less amenable to driving than it is to the south, because of the larger grains of ground-up coquina rock. A coquina shelf anchors the sand offshore and is eroded into larger granules. In a way this is a relief from the powder sand of southern Volusia, which is virtually impossible to brush off yourself without the aid of a shower. The beach around Oceanfront Park is actually one of the few stretches where the sand is hard enough to drive on—and even then you probably only want to take your car on it if you know how to avoid getting stuck.

ACCESS: From I–95, exit onto SR 40 east (Tomoka Road) and follow this all the way to the beach.

From A1A, the public beach is at Granada Boulevard and A1A in the town of Ormond Beach.

PARKING: Parking on the beach; free parking lot.

HOURS/FEES: Sunrise–sunset; free. Beach driving, November through April sunrise–sunset; May through October 8:00 A.M.–7:00 P.M. It costs $5.00 February through November.

AMENITIES: Rest rooms, showers, summer lifeguards, picnic shelter and tables, grills, boardwalk, deck.

ACTIVITIES: Picnicking, sunbathing, swimming, surfing, beach driving.

FOR MORE INFORMATION: Ormond Beach Recreation (386) 676–3250.

Volusia County Beach Services (386) 239–7873.

Bicentennial Park

The other beach park in the Ormond Beach area is north of town in Ormond-by-the-Sea—a county facility known as Bicentennial Park. Like the other fine Volusia parks, it's a spacious river-to-ocean place with countless recreational opportunities. There are courts and fields for basketball, volleyball, baseball, racquetball, soccer, football, and shuffleboard. In addition, you'll find fitness trails, and hiking trails through Florida scrub habitat.

Beach driving is virtually impossible due to the softness of the sand, and north of Ormond-by-the-Sea it's off limits completely. Adjacent to Bicentennial Park on the northern boundary is a 2-mile-long stretch of state beach known as North Peninsula State Recreation Area. There are no facilities or parking along it, but it's a wonderful undeveloped stretch of coast that you can wander off to if you want some solitude.

Just as Cocoa Beach is famous in the surfing community as the home of six-time world champion Kelly Slater, Ormond Beach is the home of four-time women's world champion Lisa Andersen. The boost Andersen has given the world of women's surfing is incalculable. For once, the male-dominated sport admitted that here was a woman who was radical by *any* standards. Interestingly enough, this area of Florida has been a breeding ground for women's talent. Four-time world champion Frieda Zamba, who dominated women's surfing in the 1980s the way Andersen did in the 1990s, hails from just up the way in Flagler Beach. The 1960s surfing legend Mimi Munro was from Ormond Beach.

ACCESS: From I–95, exit onto SR 40 east (Tomoka Road), go across the river to A1A (Ocean Shore Boulevard), turn left, and go 2.5 miles north to 1800 North Ocean Shore Boulevard.

PARKING: Free parking lot.

HOURS/FEES: Sunrise–sunset; free.

AMENITIES: Ball fields, basketball court, boardwalk, community building, fishing dock, fitness trail, nature trail, pavilion, rest rooms, showers, summer lifeguards.

ACTIVITIES: Baseball, football, basketball, volleyball, racquetball, soccer, shuffleboard, picnicking, sunbathing, swimming, surfing.

FOR MORE INFORMATION: Volusia County Beach Services (386) 239–7873.

Daytona Beach

Nearly as long as cars have been around, Daytona Beach has had them on the beaches. Before racetracks became common and when the Bonneville Salt Flats were too far out in the back of beyond to consider, the beach at Daytona was the proving ground for flat-out speed. Auto enthusiasts from all over the United States and the world came to Daytona to race their cars down the perfectly smooth surface as fast as they could make them go.

These days the speed limit is a calm 10 miles per hour, and a great deal of caution is advised given all the human traffic on the beach. Like New Smyrna, tides move water a long distance up and down the beach due to the nearly flat slope to the water's edge. During spring and fall high tides, the beaches can be occasionally closed to traffic, especially if a northeaster is blowing the water even more. In some of the extra-low tides of summer and winter, the beach expands to 200 yards wide. Beach driving follows the same rules it does throughout Volusia County: Access costs $5.00 per vehicle except in December and January, when it's free, and anything up to 33 feet long—including RVs—is allowed out on the beach.

The Daytona Beach Boardwalk is the main strip along the beachfront, where you can find arcades, shops, restaurants, and the famous Skycoaster. The latter is a 100-foot-high pendulum swing that sends you screaming toward the Atlantic at almost 60 miles per hour. For those looking for a more leisurely aerial view, the Skyride extends over the top of the quarter-mile-long Main Street Pier and costs $3.00 for a ticket. The pier is a good fishing des-

Main Street Pier at Daytona Beach.

tination as well as an entertainment center. Surfers also enjoy the waves near the pier, and a local surf cam provides live images on the Internet updated every fifteen seconds.

ACCESS: From the north or south, exit I–95 onto US 92 east (exit 87) to Daytona Beach. Follow this all the way to the beach and boardwalk.

PARKING: Parking on beach, street parking.

HOURS/FEES: Twenty-four hours for pedestrians; free. Beach driving November through April sunrise–sunset, May through October 8:00 A.M.–7:00 P.M. It costs $5.00 from February through November.

AMENITIES: Rest rooms, showers, lifeguards.

ACTIVITIES: Sunbathing, swimming, surfing, Skycoasting, fishing, beach driving, spring breaking, hog riding.

FOR MORE INFORMATION: Volusia County Beach Services (386) 239–7873.

Daytona Pier Surf Cam http://www.newsmyrnasurfcam.com/pages/daytonapier.html.

Main Street Pier (386) 253–1212.

Lighthouse Point Park

Coming down A1A from Daytona Beach, you eventually dead-end on the north side of Ponce Inlet. If you cross onto the beach at Beach Street, you can drive on the beach down to the jetty and park, or you can park at Lighthouse Point Park and walk out to the beach. The options and facilities are very similar to the situation on the south side of the inlet, though the dunes aren't as extensive. A symbiotic relationship exists between the two sides—where the north-side beach giveth away, the south-side beach taketh. The north jetty was built to provide a more dependable channel, but ended up cutting savagely into the dunes on the north bank of the inlet. All that sand ends up over on the south-side beach because there is no south jetty.

Before the north jetty was built, the inlet was wildly unpredictable, and the first attempt at a lighthouse on the south side was abandoned after a gale washed the foundations away. The Mosquito Inlet Lighthouse was finally finished in 1887 on the north side, and has been there ever since, though the inlet's name changed in 1927 to Ponce de Leon Inlet. This belated tribute to the Spanish adventurer appears to have been an attempt to sound less provincial, and more historic like Fort Matanzas and St. Augustine to the north. The lighthouse is open daily for tours.

Fishing is a good bet on the north jetty, which offers some of the best land-based fishing in northeastern Florida. The sea life is abundant around the inlet, which is why the shark population is so healthy at the moment. (See the introduction to Region 3.) Redfish, sheepshead, croaker, bluefish, and more can be expected.

Opposite page: The lighthouse at Ponce de Leon Inlet, completed in 1887.

ACCESS: From the north or south, exit I–95 onto SR 421 east (exit 85) to Port Orange, then drive east to A1A, across the river, and south on A1A to dead-end at Ponce Inlet. Beach driving access is on Beach Street.

PARKING: Parking on the beach, free street parking, parking lots at Lighthouse Point Park.

HOURS/FEES: Twenty-four hours for pedestrians; free. Lighthouse Point Park charges a $3.50 entrance fee 6:00 A.M.–9:00 P.M. Beach driving November through April sunrise–sunset, May through October 8:00 A.M.–7:00 P.M. It costs $5.00 from February through November. Ponce de Leon Inlet Lighthouse is open 10:00 A.M.–5:00 P.M.; $4.00 adults, $1.00 children under eleven.

AMENITIES: Lighthouse, fishing jetty, rest rooms, showers, nature trails, picnic pavilions.

ACTIVITIES: Sunbathing, swimming, surfing, fishing, beach driving, bird-watching, lighthouse climbing.

FOR MORE INFORMATION: Lighthouse Point Park (386) 756–7488.

Volusia County Beach Services (386) 239–7873.

Special programs/tours http://echotourism.com/programs/lighthouse.htm.

Lighthouse info http://www.ponceinlet.org.

The Turtle Man

A summer ritual in Florida is the nesting of sea turtles, which come ashore in droves on the Gulf and Atlantic Coasts. Vast stretches of undeveloped coast are ideal locations for nesting. Buildings that are lighted at night attract turtles away from the ocean after they nest, because they mistake the light for the shimmering glare of the sea. Turtles have enough natural enemies working against their successful hatching and survival without adding human ones.

At many state parks throughout the state, rangers lead night walks to observe turtles lay eggs. It's a fascinating event, watching these great creatures methodically dig a hole in the sand with their flippers, and then deposit dozens of Ping-Pong ball eggs. Once the nest is covered, the eggs are far from safe. Predators like raccoons will dig them up and destroy and entire nest in a gluttonous pig-out. If they're lucky enough to hatch and make it to the water, any number of fish are happy to eat them.

The man most responsible for the return of the turtle population to healthier numbers in Florida is Ross Witham, a native of my hometown of Stuart, Florida. There was a point when the endangered green turtle virtually disappeared from Florida, with only two nests on the entire east coast of the state. Witham, a Florida native now in his eighties, combed beaches up and down the state in search of green turtle nests to collect the eggs for a Head Start program at the Stuart House of Refuge. The eggs were incubated, hatched, and the baby turtles held in large saltwater tanks until they were big enough to stand a decent chance of survival.

Witham worked for the state Department of Natural Resources, and his hands-on work with turtles for decades made him one of the most knowledgeable people in the world on them. He traveled extensively sharing his knowledge, which was critical to the understanding and preservation of turtles throughout Florida and elsewhere. He was one of the first people to recognize that turtles have a unique homing instinct that directs them to return to the beaches where they were born—a sort of built-in GPS system that stays with them their whole lives.

Occasionally people mistook his intentions. My brother worked with him one summer, and they were digging out a nest when a woman walked by and said, "That's mean." Their heads were in the hole so they had no chance to explain themselves, and the next thing they knew she was standing on the nearby stairs hosing them down with water. Witham took such incidents in stride, though. He's a Pearl Harbor veteran and has seen more of life than most people can imagine.

Region 3

New Smyrna Beach has boomed in the past decades changing from a sleepy little beach town with dirt roads running to its southern end to a developed coastal community. The vast majority of ownership is absentee, as the area has become a favorite place for Orlando-ites to own a weekend retreat. During weekdays the town reverts to its old sleepy self. On weekends and in summer months, the beach near Ponce Inlet is quite the scene, as large numbers of Orlando residents flock to the ocean.

One slightly disturbing trend of the past few years has been the increase in shark attacks. Florida has always had shark attacks, and Volusia County gets the bulk of them, but in 2001 the county saw an unusual number and garnered national headlines. Small and aggressive blacktip sharks have been the culprit, some no more than 2 feet long, and most of the attacks occur in extremely shallow water—we're not talking *Jaws* here. The high volume of beachgoers is partly responsible for the statistics, along with murky water flowing out the inlet. Common sense will reduce the danger; just don't go into the water when you see sharks or schools of baitfish anywhere around. Many of the bites were on surfers who knew there were a lot of sharks around and went surfing anyway. Media coverage has ranged from terror hype elsewhere in the nation, causing New Smyrna Beach tourism to suffer badly, to Florida authorities insisting everything is normal. The simple truth is, the south side of Ponce Inlet has a problem. There is no reason to be unduly concerned about sharks at any other beaches in the area, or anywhere else in Florida, but caution is warranted close to the inlet.

Farther down the island at Bethune Beach, there remains a legacy to a proud chapter in Florida black history. Named after Mary McLeod Bethune, one of the most remarkable women in Florida history, the beach was similar in conception to American Beach north of Jacksonville. Rather than be denied beach access at all, or shunted off to a beach that whites designated for them, successful Daytona-area blacks bought a resort with 2.5 miles of beachfront in 1943.

Bethune had already lived an amazing life to this point, having founded the school in 1904 in Daytona that became Bethune-Cookman College, served as an education and child welfare adviser to the Coolidge, Hoover, and Roosevelt administrations, presided over the National Council of Negro Women, and became a close friend of FDR's mother, Sara, and wife, Eleanor. Her friendship with the Roosevelts led to her overseeing national conferences addressing the problems of black Americans. She wrote to Roosevelt that it had not been until that moment that there had been a "chance for Negroes themselves to suggest a comprehensive program for the full integration into the benefits and the responsibilities of American democracy." By the time of her death in 1955, she had created enormous opportunities for black Floridians and inspired blacks everywhere.

A few miles south, the road enters Canaveral National Seashore and soon dead-ends. This is the north entrance to almost 30 miles of some of the most pristine wilderness beaches in Florida, with Apollo Beach spreading out over a number of parking areas. Returning back through New Smyrna Beach to the interstate and heading south to Titusville, you can swing out to Playalinda Beach and the southern entrance to the national seashore. Once you're out on Merritt Island, it's just a short drive south to the Kennedy Space Center and all of its attractions.

Below Cape Canaveral and the entrance to the port are a number of good beaches, among them Canaveral Pier. Kelly Slater, six-time world surfing champion and occasional boyfriend of swimsuit icon Pamela Anderson, grew up in Cocoa Beach surfing the pier. An interesting area of popular surfing beaches lies in front of Patrick Air Force Base. The beaches lack much in the way of amenities beyond the odd shower or picnic table, but that doesn't stop droves of people from flocking to them for the relaxed atmosphere.

Access

From the north, take exit 84 from I–95 to New Smyrna Beach.

From the south, take exit 79 from I–95 to the Kennedy Space Center and Canaveral National Seashore.

Beaches

Smyrna Dunes Park
Bethune Beach Park
Apollo Beach—Canaveral National Seashore North
Playalinda Beach—Canaveral National Seashore South
Jetty Park
Cherie Down Park

Surfing near Patrick Air Force Base.

Canaveral Pier/Cocoa Beach
Lori Wilson Park
Patrick Air Force Base

Camping

Lake Ashby Park—(904) 428–4589, 4150 Boy Scout Camp Road, New Smyrna Beach. This sixty-four-acre park includes a boardwalk, nature trail, picnic area and pavilion, tent camping, fishing docks, horseshoes, and playground.

Apollo Beach/Canaveral National Seashore—(904) 428–3384, extension 18. Beach camping in tents only; permits can be obtained at the visitor center. Closed during summer when sea turtles are nesting. You can also camp on one of several islands in Mosquito Lagoon, with no facilities. Reservations are required. Winter months—when the mosquitos are less bothersome—are the best time to utilize these primitive sites. Boats or canoes are required to get to the lagoon campsites. Fees run $10 per night for one to six people.

Riverbreeze Park—(904) 345–2974, 250 H. H. Burch Road, Oak Hill. A boardwalk, boat ramp, camping, fishing dock, picnic area, and pavilion are available at this facility.

Jetty Park—(321) 783–7111, at the entrance to Port Canaveral in Cocoa Beach. You'll find 150 campsites here, ranging from tents to full RV hookups. May-through-December rates are $17 rustic, $21 with water/sewer, $24 with water/sewer/electric. Add $2.00 January through April.

Manatee Hammock—(321) 264–5083, 7275 South US 1, Titusville. From I–95 (exit 79), go east 3 miles on SR 50 to US 1, turn south, and go 3.5 miles. On the shore of the Indian River Lagoon, this campground is a well-shaded and quiet hammock with 147 full hookups and 30 sites with water and electric. It has a perfect view of space shuttle launches at Kennedy Space Center. Recreation, small swimming pool, grill area, fire rings, midsized pavilion, two shuffleboard courts, and a horseshoe pit. Rates are $13.75, $18.50, and $20.35 for rustic, water/electric, and full hookups, respectively.

Tosohatchee State Reserve—(407) 568–5893. West off I–95 on SR 50 along the St. Johns River. Primitive backpack camping with permit.

Wickham Park—(321) 255–4307, 2500 Parkway Drive, Melbourne. From I–95 (exit 73), take Wickham Road east 8.4 miles. After it curves around to the south, take Parkway Road east 0.5 mile. There are eighty-eight sites with water/electric, and twenty-two rustic. Two seasonally guarded swimming lakes, three small fishing lakes, an eighteen-hole disk golf course, archery range, horseshoe pits, volleyball courts, playground, multipurpose/soccer fields. Also includes exercise trail, nature trails, and horse trails. Rates are $12.10 rustic, $16.23 water/electric.

Other Points of Interest

Kennedy Space Center—(407) 452–2121, east of Titusville on SR 405/NASA Parkway. One of the most popular attractions in Florida. Open daily 9:00 A.M.–dusk, except Christmas Day. Free admission for the center. Bus tours are $14 for adults and $10 for children ages three through eleven (in U.S. dollars). With an IMAX film, the price is $19 adults, $15 children. Launch updates at (800) 572–4636, and bus passes for shuttle launches are $10. There is an enormous amount to see here, so if you don't want to go the bus tour route, spend some time at the visitor center plotting your day.

U.S. Astronaut Hall of Fame—(407) 269–6100. Memorabilia from forty-four astronauts and hands-on activities. Take a simulated moon walk, land the space shuttle via a video screen, and feel what four g's of pull does to your body. Open daily 9:00 A.M.–5:00 P.M.; admission is $13.95 adults, $9.95 children.

Brevard County Museum of History and Natural Science—(321) 632–1830, a few miles west of Cocoa Beach at 2201 Michigan Avenue. Displays recount the area's origins as a trading post; there are also archaeological and wildlife exhibits, and walking tours through Olde Cocoa Village. Tuesday through Saturday 10:00 A.M.–4:00 P.M., and Sunday 1:00–4:00 P.M.

Merritt Island National Wildlife Refuge—(407) 861–0667. Huge area of wetlands and nature on the way out to Playalinda Beach. The visitor center is open Monday through Saturday during daylight hours April through October, and also on Sunday 9:00 A.M.–5:00 P.M. November through March. Closed within twenty-four hours of a space shuttle launch.

Hontoon Island State Park—(904) 736–5309, west from New Smyrna Beach on SR 44; 6 miles west of DeLand. This island bordered by the St. Johns River and Hontoon Dead River is accessible by free passenger ferry. Cabins, camping, and lots of recreation. The entrance fee is $3.25.

Cocoa Beach Surfing School—(321) 868–1980, www.ronjons.com, 150 East Columbia Lane, Cocoa Beach. Learn to surf in the town that produced six-time world champion Kelly Slater.

Jetty Park.

Region 3

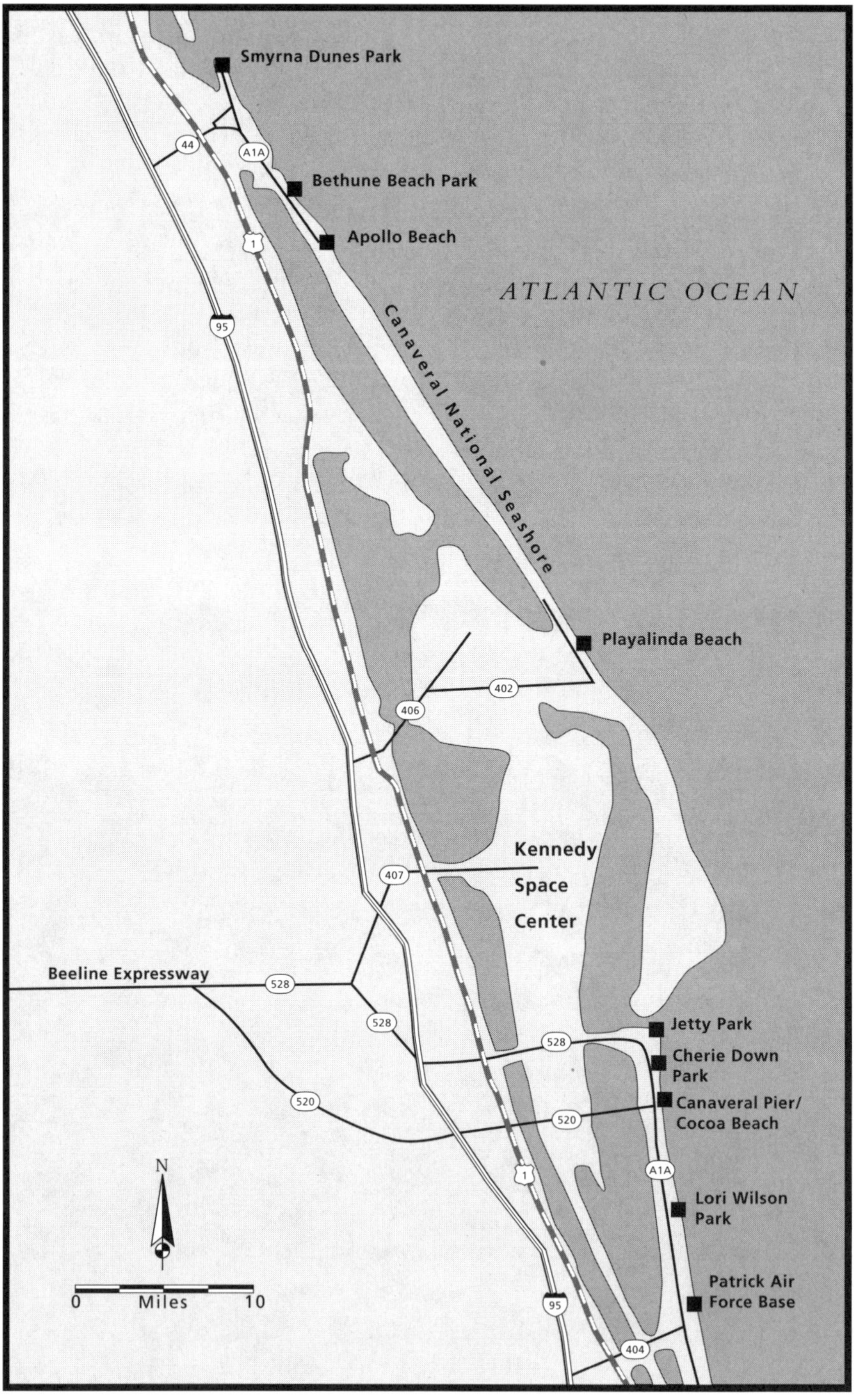

Smyrna Dunes Park
44
A1A
Bethune Beach Park
Apollo Beach
1
ATLANTIC OCEAN
95
Canaveral National Seashore
Playalinda Beach
402
406
Kennedy
Space
Center
407
Beeline Expressway
528
528
528
Jetty Park
Cherie Down
Park
520
520
Canaveral Pier/
Cocoa Beach
A1A
1
Lori Wilson
Park
N
0
Miles
10
95
Patrick Air
Force Base
404

Smyrna Dunes Park

The south side of Ponce Inlet in New Smyrna Beach is a beautiful stretch of beach, and one of the premier surf zones of the east coast of Florida. Because it picks up southeast swells that the coast farther south does not, sometimes it seems like the entire surfing population of Florida has descended upon it. There has long been a thriving local surf community, and some great talent has emerged from "The Inlet." There is no south jetty, and surfers on the northern bars are surfing almost in the middle of the inlet.

There are many reasons to come to the beach here, and a couple of different ways to access it. You can drive your car on the beach, accessing it from various crossovers 0.5 mile or more to the south. From February through November, there is a $5.00 fee to drive on the beach; it's always

Smyrna Dunes Park.

open and free to pedestrians and bicyclists. The old, old days of setting speed records on the beach are long gone, and it's important to obey the speed limits and keep a careful eye out for sunbathers. The local police enforce the beach driving laws quite strictly. Park facing the dune or ocean, and stay on the east (ocean) side of the boundary posts so as not to disturb the dunes. Also keep an eye on where the high-tide line is. The beach slope is so gentle here that the incoming tide comes a long way up the beach.

The other way to access the beach is through Smyrna Dunes Park. This exquisite 250-acre park runs from the Mosquito Lagoon side around to Ponce Inlet and fronts on the Atlantic. A 2-mile boardwalk, which includes an observation tower, winds through coastal forest, salt marsh, and out across the fragile sand dunes to the beach. There are shady picnic facilities and rest rooms at the beach end. Pets are allowed but must be kept on a leash. Guided nature walks take place every Saturday morning at 11:00 A.M.

ACCESS: From the north or south, take exit 84 from I–95 to SR 44 east and drive 5 miles to either North or South Causeway. Turn left onto Peninsula Avenue after crossing the causeway, then continue north 2 or 3 miles to Smyrna Dunes Park. For beach driving access, turn right off Peninsula Avenue onto Inlet Street.

PARKING: Parking on the beach, free street parking, parking lots at Smyrna Dunes Park.

HOURS/FEES: Twenty-four hours for pedestrians; free. Smyrna Dunes Park charges a $3.50 vehicle entrance fee 6:00 A.M.–7:00 P.M.; in summer, 6:00 A.M.–8:00 P.M. Beach driving November through April sunrise–sunset, May through October 8:00 A.M.–7:00 P.M. It costs $5.00 February through November.

AMENITIES: Rest rooms, showers, boardwalk, picnic pavilions, nature trails, observation tower.

ACTIVITIES: Sunbathing, swimming, surfing, fishing, beach driving, bird-watching.

FOR MORE INFORMATION: Smyrna Dunes Park (386) 424–2935.

Volusia County Beach Services (386) 239–7873.

Bethune Beach Park

This is a fantastic beach park toward the end of New Smyrna Beach, shortly before you reach the Canaveral National Seashore boundaries. The park occupies both sides of A1A and includes basketball and tennis courts, along with a nature trail and a fitness trail. Fishing docks grace the river. People who aren't going to the national seashore often don't get down this far, because beach access appears to be limited by condo development for most of the way down here past where SR 44 meets A1A. The park is something of a local secret, especially on weekends and in summertime when the beaches close to Ponce Inlet are teeming with people.

The beach at Bethune Beach Park is part of the Natural Zone designation of Volusia County beaches, which means driving on it is not allowed. For people who can't handle the car scene of the beaches to the north in peak season, this prohibition is another draw. Swimming is good in the summer and at other times of year when it's calm, but currents can be dangerous when it's rough. Surfers, particularly longboarders, enjoy the relaxed atmosphere here compared to the hypercompetitive scene up by the inlet. Extensive facilities, great beach, easy parking, and it's free—a rare and wonderful combination.

ACCESS: From the north or south, take exit 84 off I–95 to SR 44 east, go 7 miles to A1A south, then continue 5 miles south on A1A to the park.

PARKING: Free parking lot.

HOURS/FEES: Twenty-four hours; free.

AMENITIES: Lifeguards, rest rooms, boardwalk, community building, fishing docks, fitness trail, nature trail, playground, basketball and tennis courts.

ACTIVITIES: Sunbathing, swimming, surfing, fishing, tennis, basketball, hiking, jogging.

FOR MORE INFORMATION: Mary McLeod Bethune Beach Park (386) 736–5953.

Apollo Beach—Canaveral National Seashore North

The main beach at the northern end of Canaveral National Seashore, Apollo Beach, offers the same seemingly limitless expanse of empty beach as Playalinda Beach does at the southern end. Beginning just past the entrance station, the access to the beach is strung out in five parking lots and walkovers along a 5-mile section. Beach camping is allowed at a site 400 yards south of Lot 1, and another site 400 yards south of the dune walkover at the visitor center. Backcountry camping is possible on eleven designated islands in Mosquito Lagoon, as well as on the 15 miles of wilderness beach between Apollo and Playalinda that is accessible only by foot or boat. Permits are required and cost $10 per night for groups up to six people.

Two miles south of the visitor center—which is near the entrance—is the Eldora State House. The loop road to Eldora veers off the main beach road,

Eldora House at Canaveral National Seashore.

and a sand trail runs a quarter mile to the house. The historic home is open only on weekends at the moment, 10:00 A.M.–4:00 P.M., and features exhibits and information about the community of Eldora. The small town existed from 1877 to 1914, and was an important stopping point along the river for shippers and tourists on nineteenth-century riverboats. Eldora House was one of the larger houses built in the early days, and served as a hotel for a while. Jonathan Dickinson would have welcomed the hotel had it existed a few centuries earlier, because it was along this stretch of coast that his group suffered most horribly. (See Region 5 for Dickinson's saga.)

Henry Flagler's railroad took away much of the shipping business after the turn of the twentieth century, and the opening of the Intracoastal Waterway on the west side of the lagoon gave Eldora little reason for existence anymore. When the national seashore was established in 1975, there wasn't much left of Eldora except the old house known as both Eldora House and State House, and it became a museum to preserve the history of the town. In 1999 it was completely renovated, and is in fine condition. There is a fishing dock near the house, where you can fish in the lagoon without a license.

Boat ramps are located right near the entrance, and there are boat docks at the visitor center. A pontoon boat takes visitors for a two-hour tour through the lagoon with a park ranger as a guide; it's a great way to learn the interesting history of the area. Tours go out on Friday through Sunday, weather permitting, and cost $13 per person. Mosquito Lagoon provides some extraordinary fishing for redfish and trout.

ACCESS: From the north or south, take exit 84 off I–95 to SR 44 east and go 7 miles to A1A, then south on A1A for 7 miles to Canaveral National Seashore entrance; it's 2 miles farther to Apollo Beach.

PARKING: Free parking lots.

HOURS/FEES: 6:00 A.M.–6:00 P.M.; $5.00 entrance fee.

AMENITIES: Summer lifeguards, rest rooms, dune walkovers, museum.

ACTIVITIES: Swimming, surfing, fishing, beach walking, nature viewing, river tours, backcountry camping.

FOR MORE INFORMATION: Visitor information (386) 428–3384; www.nps.gov/cana/.

Boat tour reservations (386) 428–3384, ext. 10.

Playalinda Beach—Canaveral National Seashore South

With a name that translates from the Spanish as "pretty beach," it's something of a wonder that this beach on Canaveral National Seashore is the only one in Florida so called. There could not be a more deserving one, though. The Canaveral National Seashore is one of the greatest gems of conservation on the Florida coast, spanning 30 miles of completely undeveloped natural Florida beach. Playalinda Beach is the 4 miles accessible from the southern end, lying in the shadow of the space shuttle launch pads at Kennedy Space Center. Because the beach is so close to the shuttle launches, for security reasons the beach is closed for three days before a shuttle launch and opened again the day after a successful shuttle launch. For information on these dates, you can look at either the CNS Web site or the Kennedy Space Center Web site.

Starting at the southern parking area, Lot 1, there are miles and miles of empty beach you can walk along to the south toward False Cape, passing right by the enormous launch pads. Heading north by road to the other parking areas, there are thirteen lots to choose from along a 4-mile stretch until you reach the final one. North of Lot 13 is where the unofficial nude beach begins. There have been random crackdowns over the years, but the last major one was in 1993.

Jutting much farther out into the Atlantic than beaches in Cocoa and Melbourne, Playalinda is open to swells from almost any direction. Because it's a long way off the beaten path without nearby food options, surprisingly few surfers come here. The most popular it gets is when hurricane swells are coming from far to the southwest of the Bahamas, and everywhere south of the cape is being blocked from the surf. There is so much room to spread out in the surf, though, that it's never crowded.

ACCESS: From the north or south, take exit 80 off I–95 onto SR 406 east to Titusville. Cross the Max Brewer Causeway to Merritt Island National Wildlife Refuge; where the road forks, stay to the right on SR 402 until you reach the entrance gate to Canaveral National Seashore. Playalinda Beach begins where road reaches the coast and parallels it for 4 miles.

PARKING: Thirteen parking lots.

HOURS/FEES: 6:00 A.M.–6:00 P.M., $5.00 entrance fee.

AMENITIES: Summer lifeguards, rest rooms, dune walkovers.

ACTIVITIES: Swimming, surfing, fishing, beach walking, nature viewing, unofficial nude sunbathing.

FOR MORE INFORMATION: Canaveral National Seashore (321) 267–1110; www.nps.gov/cana/.

Surf conditions/closures (321) 867–2805.

Kennedy Space Center (321) 452–2121; www.ksc.com.

Nude beach status www.central-fla-naturists.org.

Jetty Park

Port Canaveral is the only cruise ship port north of Palm Beach, taking advantage of its proximity to Orlando to draw vacationers. There are dreams of linking Port Canaveral with Orlando by high-speed rail, but they are unlikely to become reality anytime soon. A thirty-five-acre beach park occupies the south side of the port entrance, including the 1,200-foot-long fishing jetty that is paved for easy access. The beach is wide, and is one of the best places for viewing shuttle launches in the area. Everyone knows this, though, so you have to get there early to make sure you get a parking spot. It's an incredibly popular park because of the variety of facilities, with a large campground and nearby free public boat ramps. On the other side of the port channel is a docking bay for Trident submarines, so you never know what you might see coming or going.

ACCESS: From the north, take exit 77 off I–95 to SR 528 (Beeline Expressway) east; go across both bridges to the coast, taking the Port Canaveral exit, and follow signs to Jetty Park.

From the south, take exit 75 off I–95 onto SR 520 east; go all the way to the coast, turn left onto A1A, and go 3 miles north to Jetty Park.

PARKING: Parking lots.

HOURS/FEES: Twenty-four hours; $3.00 per car, $7.00 per RV.

AMENITIES: Fishing jetty, showers, rest rooms, picnic tables, campground, bait and tackle shop.

ACTIVITIES: Sunbathing, swimming, fishing, shuttle launch viewing, ship-watching.

FOR MORE INFORMATION: Canaveral Port Authority (321) 783–7831.

Cherie Down Park

Behind the local elementary school in the town of Cape Canaveral, this quiet park has an expansive beach that seems to double in width at lower tides. The waters are so shallow near shore that at high tide you can splash around for a long time before getting more than knee deep, and the beach is guarded in summer months. A boardwalk runs along the dunes from one end to the other. The beach is perfect for games of volleyball or chasing Frisbees into the water. With Jetty Park and Canaveral Pier to the north and south picking up the brunt of the beachgoers, Cherie Down is a nice place to get away from the crowds. The dunes and sea oats remain intact, making it one of the more natural beaches in a fairly developed stretch of coastline.

ACCESS: From the north, take exit 77 off I–95 to SR 528 (Beeline Expressway) east. Go to the coast and stay on A1A south. In the town of Cape Canaveral, look for Ridgewood Avenue on your left; the park is behind Cape View Elementary.

From the south, take exit 75 from I–95 onto SR 520 east. Go all the way to the coast. Turn left onto A1A and go 2.5 miles to Ridgewood Avenue, on your right.

PARKING: Parking lot.

HOURS/FEES: 7:00 A.M.–sunset; free.

AMENITIES: Showers, rest rooms, summer lifeguards, pavilion, picnic shelters, boardwalk.

ACTIVITIES: Sunbathing, swimming, fishing, surfing.

FOR MORE INFORMATION: Brevard Parks (321) 455–1380; www.brevardparks.com.

Canaveral Pier/Cocoa Beach

Known as both the Canaveral Pier and the Cocoa Beach Pier, this venerable structure protruding 800 feet into the Atlantic is one of the centers of beach life on the Space Coast. It has existed since 1962, and is one of the closest things Florida has to the full commercial style of beach pier, with dozens of shops and restaurants to go along with the fishing and surfing. The pier was home to pioneering east coast surfer Gary Propper in the 1960s, who went on to make a fortune as the man who invented Teenage Mutant Ninja Turtles. The pier is still home to two major surfing competitions each year: the thirty-six-year-old Easter Surfing Festival, and the Labor Day Surfing Festival, which benefits the National Kidney Foundation. Memorial Day weekend brings the Beachfest, a huge annual music festival that is attended by tens of thousands.

The Beeline Expressway leads directly from Orlando to Cocoa Beach, so it's the quickest way for Orlando residents to get to the beach. There's plenty of sand for frolicking, and the slope into the water is very gradual so it's a

Canaveral Pier.

fairly safe place to swim. The waves break a good distance from shore to shallow sandbars, and there is rarely a problem with rip currents close to the beach. Rod and reel rentals are available on the pier; there's always something biting. With the space shuttle launch pads less than 10 miles away, the pier is also one of the prime spots to watch a shuttle launch from.

ACCESS: From the north, take exit 77 off I–95 onto SR 528 (Beeline Expressway) east. Go all the way to the coast where it merges with A1A; 0.5 mile south is Meade Avenue. Turn left to the pier.

From the south, take exit 75 off I–95 onto SR 520 east. Go all the way to the coast, turn left onto A1A, and go 0.5 mile north to Meade Avenue. Turn right to the pier.

PARKING: Metered parking near the pier.

HOURS/FEES: Twenty-four hours; free.

AMENITIES: Fishing pier, lifeguards, showers, rest rooms, restaurants, shops.

ACTIVITIES: Sunbathing, swimming, surfing, volleyball, fishing, shopping, picnicking.

FOR MORE INFORMATION: Cocoa Beach Pier (321) 783–7549; www.l-n.com/cocoa.beach.pier.

Lori Wilson Park

This beach is a pleasant surprise in the middle of the town of Cocoa Beach, because while the beaches along the Space Coast themselves tend to be uniformly nice, there don't tend to be that many natural settings. The park has a 300-foot boardwalk through a thick maritime hammock, along with a nature center to learn about the kind of trees that make up these coastal forests. On the Space Coast south of the Canaveral National Seashore, this is one of the only remaining coastal hammocks in existence. Overlooking the beach is another long boardwalk connecting to all the dune crossovers; lifeguards patrol in summer. Picnicking or grilling is a good way to spend the afternoon at the north end of the park, where sand volleyball and horseshoe courts are set up. Pavilions throughout the area offer shade.

ACCESS: From I–95, take exit 75 onto SR 520 east. Go all the way to the coast, turn left onto A1A (Atlantic Avenue), and go 3.5 miles south.

From A1A, access is in the middle of town of Cocoa Beach at 1500 Atlantic Avenue.

PARKING: Parking lots.

HOURS/FEES: 7:00 A.M.–sunset; free.

AMENITIES: Nature center, pavilions, grills, summer lifeguards, showers, rest rooms, sand volleyball court, boardwalk, maritime hammock.

ACTIVITIES: Sunbathing, swimming, fishing, surfing, nature study, horseshoes, volleyball.

FOR MORE INFORMATION: Johnnie Johnson Nature Center (321) 868–1123.

Brevard Parks (321) 455–1380; www.brevardparks.com.

Patrick Air Force Base

Coming south, this area features some of the first underlying stratas of coquina rock, which you see much more spectacular raised examples of on the lower Treasure Coast. Depending on the prevailing sand shifts, the rock can be exposed in the shallows, making caution necessary getting in and out of the water. The first dirt parking lot on the left as you approach from Cocoa Beach on A1A is a place known as Picnic Tables. There's substantial parking, and a pavilion with picnic tables, showers, and rest rooms. The facilities are provided by the base, and are some of the only rest rooms available along this stretch.

In between this lot and the next parking area south are the busy surf breaks First Light and Second Light, though there's no longer a traffic light at First Light. The next parking lot is a spot called Hangars, named—in the obvious way surfers do—after the large airplane hangar across the street at the base. It's located just a short distance north of the beachside NCO club. As any enlisted man would tell you, the noncommissioned officers actually run everything in the military despite what the higher brass might think, and this prize piece of real estate is reflective of that. There are no facilities at Hangars, just more nice beach and the old site of Patrick Pier. Underwater pilings can still be a hazard right here, so for safer swimming waters it's better to go down the beach a little.

A county park, South Patrick Resident Association Park, is 1.5 miles south of the base and Pineda Causeway. It has a shower and dune walkovers, along with a Challenger Memorial in tribute to the doomed space shuttle.

ACCESS: From the north, take exit 73 off I–95 onto SR 509/Wickham Road east. Go to SR 404/Pineda Causeway, cross the river to A1A, then go north to the surf beaches and 1.5 miles south to the South Patrick Resident Association Park.

From the south, the park is 5 miles north of Melbourne Causeway/US 192 on A1A.

PARKING: Free lots.

HOURS/FEES: Sunrise–sunset.

AMENITIES: Showers, rest rooms, picnic tables.

ACTIVITIES: Sunbathing, swimming, surfing, picnicking.

FOR MORE INFORMATION: Brevard County Parks (321) 952–4650; www.brevardparks.com.

Satellite Beach Skatepark (321) 777–3538.

Surfing at Hangars.

Shuttle Launches

You can reduce life to its barest essentials here on the cape, or you can marvel at the highest technology humankind has created, but alas, you can't do both at the same time. The Kennedy Space Center is fairly strict about visitors keeping their clothes on while touring the complex, and the surrounding beaches are closed within twenty-four hours of a rocket or space shuttle launch.

From the Treasure Coast up to Jacksonville, shuttle launches are an integral part of Florida culture. People stop what they're doing to watch the exhaust trail curve its way across the sky, sending another group of astronauts into orbit. No matter how many times it happens or how accustomed we become to the idea of humans in space, it is still a marvel to behold. Viewed from up close at Jetty Park on the south side of Port Canaveral, or by obtaining a pass to view it from a site on NASA property, night launches contain a special majesty. The contrast of fire against black night, of such stunning power overcoming the bonds of gravity, cannot fail to take your breath away.

Kennedy Space Center.

Region 4

The Melbourne area juxtaposes modern beach culture with a caught-in-time 1950s ambience that it has never quite shed. As the hub of the east coast surfing industry, Melbourne is the best place to get surfing equipment in Florida. It's still a low-key area, except when Orlando invades on the weekends. Jim Jarmusch set part of his film *Stranger than Paradise* in Melbourne, and the old-time look of pastel motels still lives on along A1A. The Melbourne International Airport—which justifies its rather grand title on the basis of flights to the Bahamas—is actually drawing more carriers these days, and Spirit Airlines flies regularly now between Melbourne and the northeastern United States.

Pelican Beach Park is the best of Satellite Beach public beaches, though surfers favor the nearby big-wave spot known as "RC's" when the swell really booms. Local surfer Bill Hartley rode a 9-foot, 6-inch Hawaiian big-wave board there on the fabled Halloween swell of 1990 that came from *The Perfect Storm* of the book and movie. Down in Indialantic the boardwalk is the popular hangout. South of Ocean Avenue on the edge of Melbourne, Spessard Holland Park is among less developed offerings, and has a public golf course associated with it.

As you approach Sebastian Inlet, Long Point Park is on the river side of the road with a dirt parking lot by A1A, and trails through the woods to the beach. At the Sebastian Inlet State Park, a legendary surf break by the north jetty—First Peak—is known throughout the international surfing community, and numerous competitions have been held there over the years. The Treasure Coast begins on the south side of the inlet. Some amazing bounties have been pulled from shipwrecks just off the beach.

The misfortunes of the treasure fleets were what gave the coast its name. Most famous of these was the 1715 fleet, the story of which is told at the McLarty Treasure Museum at Sebastian Inlet. Between the inlet and Wabasso Beach, the coast is still very wild. Soon it becomes tamed by development, which blocks access through most of the county except in the city of Vero Beach. There are more beaches than are readily apparent driving along A1A, but they don't leap out at you. Tracking Station Park, Jaycee Park, and South Beach Park comprise the city beaches, and little access is available until you leave Indian River County.

The island becomes wild again, with little development south of the county line. The long stretch of state beach at Avalon is appealing to the solitary soul; it's just north of the excellent county park at Pepper Beach. Claude Pepper, a legendary Florida public servant, was its namesake. Pepper served the people for an astonishing breadth of time, first in the state legislature in 1929, then as a U.S. senator from 1937 to 1951, during which time he was a strong liberal ally of Roosevelt. After suffering persecution by Joseph McCarthy, he returned to Congress as a House member from 1963 to his death in 1989. He championed the rights of the elderly in his final twenty years—a relentless battler.

Like Sebastian, a huge area on the north side of Fort Pierce Inlet is devoted to a state park, and it's another popular surfing and swimming area. The Navy Underwater Demolition Team used the entire south end of the island as a training area during World War II. It was the birthplace of the UDT, which eventually transformed into the Navy SEALs of today. A mile to the north of the recreation area is the UDT–Navy SEALs Museum, which contains a great history of navy frogmen. The Navy SEAL from the *Survivor* TV show, Rudy, has some of his gear on display there. Don't worry, though; the beaches are as safe as can be these days.

Access

From the north on I–95, take exit 72 to SR 518 east. Cross the Eau Gallie Causeway to A1A.

From the south on I–95, take exit 66 to SR 68 east to US 1. Turn left and go 3 miles to A1A north.

Beaches

Pelican Beach Park
Indialantic Boardwalk
Spessard Holland Park
Long Point Park
Sebastian Inlet State Park
Jaycee Park
South Beach Park
Avalon

Pepper Beach County Park
Fort Pierce Inlet State Park

Camping

Sebastian Inlet State Park—(772) 589–9659. The park has fifty-one sites with electricity and water overlooking the south side of the inlet. Fees are $13 from May through November, and $17 from December through April.

Long Point Park—(321) 952–4532, www.brevardparks.com. There are a hundred riverfront campsites on the Indian river just a few hundred yards from the beach, plus twelve RV sites with full hookups.

KOA Kampground—(772) 589–5665, 8850 US 1, Wabasso 32970. RVs and tent camping sites. Facilities include bathrooms, activity building, electrical hookups, swimming pool, and laundry room.

Other Points of Interest

Brevard Zoo—(321) 254–WILD, Wickham Road at exit 73 off I–95, Melbourne; info@brevardzoo.org; http://www.brevardzoo.org/. The only zoo in the United States to offer kayaking tours. Features a mini train, alligator and crocodile feedings, elevated boardwalks through tropical tree hammock, and a wide variety of animals native to Latin America and Florida—llamas, rheas, giant anteaters, tapirs, monkeys, exotic birds, alligators, crocodiles, river otters, bald eagles, red wolves, and more. *Australia Exhibit* features a free flight aviary with cockatoos, lorikeets, budgeriagars, and laughing kookaburras along with an Outback habitat of red kangaroo, emu, and wallaby. The recently opened *Flying Fox Forest* features giant fruit bats, many exotic species of birds, muntjac, and a beautiful orchid garden. Open 10:00 A.M.–5:00 P.M.

Satellite Beach Skatepark—(321) 777–3538. Follow signs to Satellite Beach Library from A1A. An outdoor concrete skatepark run by the town of Satellite Beach. The fee is $3.00.

Sebastian Inlet Marina—(321) 724–5424, just north of the inlet on the Indian River. Fishing charters and party boat fishing are available. The deepwater reef fishing is excellent offshore; flats fishing in the Indian River for redfish and snook is also great.

Pelican Island National Wildlife Refuge—(800) 952–1126, on Indian River south of Sebastian Inlet. The first designated national wildlife refuge in the United States, with large rookeries and a variety of bird life. Tours are available on a forty-nine-passenger boat out of Sebastian Inlet Marina.

Dodgertown—(772) 569–4900, just north of SR 60 west of I–95 in Vero Beach. Catch a spring training game of the Los Angeles Dodgers at Holman Stadium.

UDT–Navy SEAL Museum—(772) 595–1570. At Pepper Beach on A1A in Fort Pierce. The history of the navy's frogmen and their training in this area.

A. E. "Beanie" Backus Gallery—(772) 465–0630. On Indian River Drive by the South Causeway in Fort Pierce. Home to the work of Florida's greatest landscape painter, who was a friend of the writer Zora Neale Hurston and a local character.

Jaycee Park, Vero Beach.

Region 4

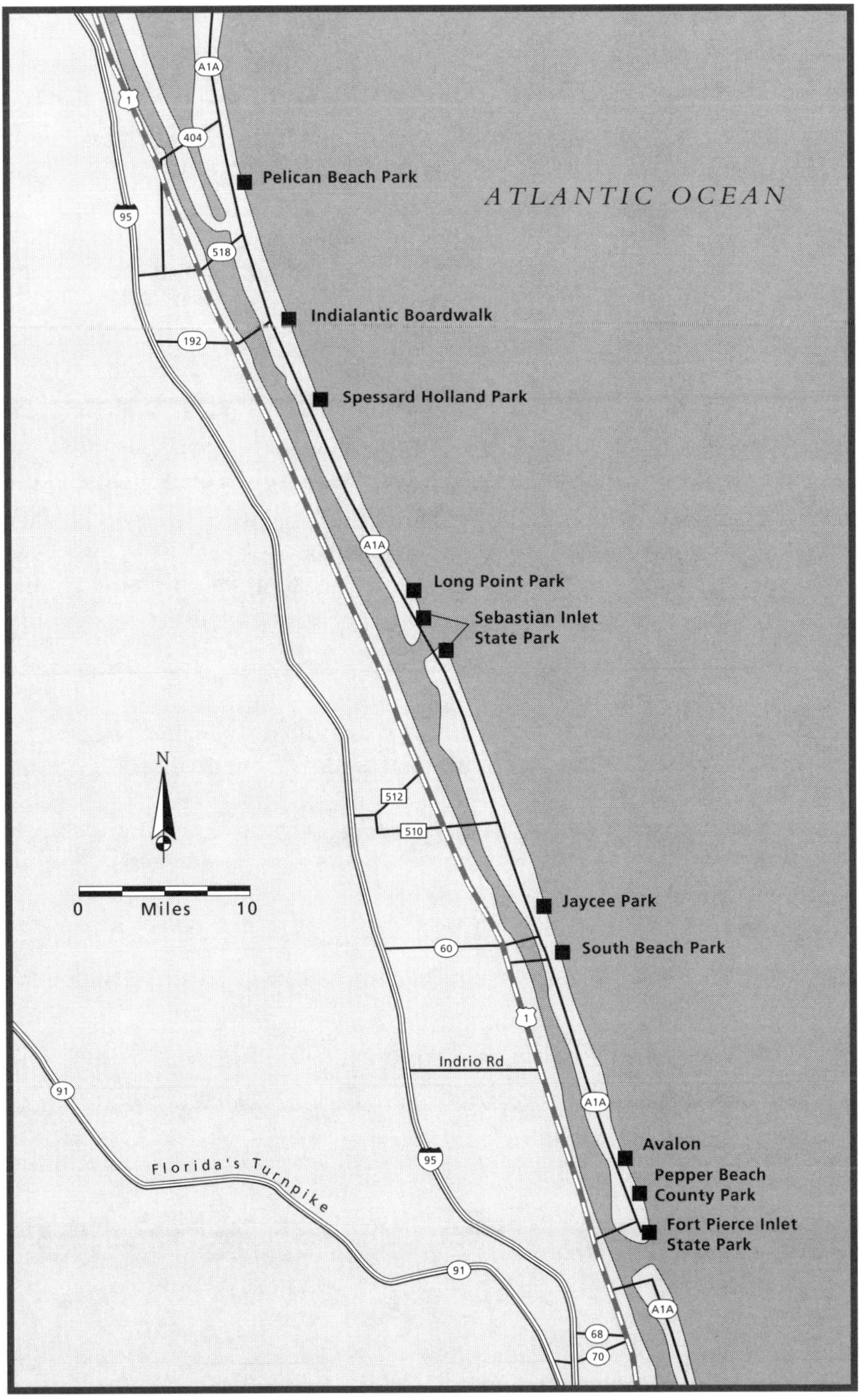

A1A
1
404
Pelican Beach Park
ATLANTIC OCEAN
95
518
Indialantic Boardwalk
192
Spessard Holland Park
A1A
Long Point Park
Sebastian Inlet
State Park
N
512
510
0 Miles 10
Jaycee Park
60
South Beach Park
1
Indrio Rd
91
A1A
Avalon
95
Florida's Turnpike
Pepper Beach
County Park
Fort Pierce Inlet
State Park
91
A1A
68
70

Pelican Beach Park

Another of the easily accessed beaches from the Orlando area, this is typical of the area's wide strands with shallow water near shore. Surfers tend to favor the waves just up to the north at Patrick Air Force Base, but swimmers and youngsters enjoy the mellower conditions here. The free parking is certainly a bonus, but as you might expect, you don't get lifeguards. It's a nice fishing beach, and surfcasters are a common sight.

Within the town of Satellite Beach and run by the city, the county-owned piece of land features high dunes with dense growths of sea grape trees, along with two boardwalks leading down to the beach. The southern one is wheelchair accessible. The scenery is refreshing as one of the few stretches of classic, unimproved Florida native coast available in this area.

Nearby is the Satellite Beach Library, and there is a public outdoor skatepark located a few hundred yards from its doors. If it gets too hot at the beach, you can cool down in the air-conditioning, read a book, and send the kids off to skate. Another stone's throw leads you to the warehouse of Greg Loehr, a great surfing and surfboard-making legend in Florida. One of the mad scientists of the surfing industry, Greg has always been on the cutting edge of improvements in resins and foams, taking advantage of the proximity of NASA and space program technology.

ACCESS: From the north, exit I–95 onto SR 518/Royal Palm Boulevard east. Follow this to A1A, turn left, and go 2.5 miles north.

From the south, the park is 3.5 miles north of the Melbourne Causeway/US 192 on A1A.

PARKING: Two hundred parking spaces.

HOURS/FEES: Dawn–dusk.

AMENITIES: Showers, rest rooms, concessions, picnic tables, observation tower.

ACTIVITIES: Sunbathing, swimming, surfing, picnicking.

FOR MORE INFORMATION: Brevard County Parks (321) 952–4650; www.brevardparks.com.

Satellite Beach Skatepark (321) 777–3538.

Indialantic Boardwalk

This pleasant, popular beach in the heart of the Melbourne area has a lot of parking—and the US 192 causeway from the mainland empties right into it. Just off the beach are a number of surf shops and a thriving commercial district. The slope into the water is very gentle, making it a favorite for wading and family play.

The beach is quite busy on weekends, when the inland population of Orlando floods out to the Melbourne area. It's also the summer hub of life in Melbourne, a mix of bikini-clad ladies, parents, senior citizens, and surfing grommets. A number of Florida pro surfers have gotten their start in the shorebreak at the boardwalk, including an aerial wizard named Jon Holeman who was doing bizarre tricks in my own days of competitive surfing, ten years before the rest of the surfing world started adopting them. The waves aren't terribly good—just a ferocious shorebreak to surf at high tide that hones your reflexes to razor sharpness.

Indialantic itself has long been a hub of Florida surfing, and is home to *Eastern Surf* magazine. It's funny that such a low-key community has maintained such a thriving surf scene over the years, especially since there are few good surf breaks in the area, but tradition goes a long way.

ACCESS: From the north, take exit 71 off I–95 southbound onto US 192 east. Follow this across the Melbourne Causeway to A1A and out to the dead end at the beach.

From the south, the park is 1.5 miles north of Ocean Avenue/ Melbourne Beach on A1A.

PARKING: Four hundred metered parking spaces along length of boardwalk.

HOURS/FEES: Sunrise–9:00 P.M.; 25 cents for each twenty minutes of metered parking.

AMENITIES: Showers, rest rooms, summer lifeguards, picnic tables, boardwalk.

ACTIVITIES: Volleyball, swimming, surfing, picnicking.

FOR MORE INFORMATION: Indialantic Town Hall (321) 723–2242.

Spessard Holland Park

One of the nicer beaches in the Melbourne area, Spessard Holland is a quiet county park. Located a couple of miles south of the slight jog in A1A at Ocean Avenue, the long strip of sea oat dunes and grainy sand extends for a mile. There are north and south entrances a half mile apart, with pavilions for picnicking and good-sized parking lots. Lifeguards are on duty during summer months. The south park has a small boardwalk and is the slightly larger of the two, though you're welcome to the entire beach in between.

Across the street from the south park is the Spessard Holland Golf Course, where you can get eighteen holes of golf from April through November for less than $17. Check out golfspacecoast.com for winter fees.

ACCESS: From the north, take exit 71 off I–95 onto US 192 east. Follow this across the Melbourne Causeway to A1A, turn right onto A1A, and go 3 miles south.

From the south, the park is 14 miles north of Sebastian Inlet on A1A.

PARKING: You'll find 180 spaces in two lots, north and south.

HOURS/FEES: 7:30 A.M.–sundown; free.

AMENITIES: Showers, rest rooms, pavilions, picnic tables, golf course, summer lifeguards.

ACTIVITIES: Swimming, surfing, picnicking, volleyball, golf.

FOR MORE INFORMATION: Brevard County Parks (407) 952–4650; www.brevardparks.com.

Spessard Holland Golf Course (321) 952–4530; pro shop info (321) 952–4529.

Golf fees
www.golfspacecoast.com/brevard/spessardholland/spessfees.html.

Long Point Park

The beach out on the ocean side of Long Point Park is ostensibly part of the Sebastian Inlet State Park land, but there is no fee to use it. The beach has been traditionally known by surfers as Spanish House, after a stucco-roofed house that used to be the first sign of development north of Sebastian Inlet. In the past there was roadside parking all along here, but that was eradicated; now there's a small dirt lot at the turnoff to Long Point Park and the Sebastian Inlet Marina. The parking is free, but it is limited and fills up quickly.

A sandy pathway leads through the dense coastal forest out to the beach, which is an undeveloped piece of beauty that runs all the way down to the north jetty of Sebastian Inlet. The offshore sandbars vary through the seasons, sometimes producing the best waves in the area.

Wood storks.

On the Indian River is an 84.5-acre conservation area on an island, which is Long Point Park. This is one of Brevard County's nicest parks, with over one hundred waterfront campsites with water and electric, and more than a dozen full hookups for RV camping. The park is a favorite of fishermen, who can fish right from their campsites, use the fishing dock, or launch a boat from the boat ramp. Otters, bobcats, herons, and manatees may be seen around the island, and the park is also a roosting site for wood storks. Adjacent to the main park and connected by a walking bridge, Scout Island offers a primitive camping area with more than a mile of nature trails.

ACCESS: From the north, take exit 71 off I–95 southbound onto US 192 east. Follow this across the Melbourne Causeway to A1A, turn right onto A1A, and go 17 miles. Parking is on your right 1 mile before Sebastian Inlet.

From the south, exit I–95 northbound onto Fellsmere Road east. Within 5 miles look for CR 510 on your right. Follow 510 all the way to the coast and A1A; turn left onto A1A and go past Sebastian Inlet for a mile. The parking area will be on your left.

PARKING: Free lot on the west side of A1A.

HOURS/FEES: Twenty-four hours; free.

AMENITIES: No amenities.

ACTIVITIES: Surfing, fishing, camping, swimming, sunbathing.

FOR MORE INFORMATION: Long Point Park (321) 952–4532; www.brevardparks.com.

Sebastian Inlet State Park, North Side

The north side of Sebastian Inlet is most famous for its surfing. The level of competition is so great, and the crowds so thick, that *infamous* is perhaps the best word to describe the surfing by the jetty. When surf magazine editors like to throw out an extreme example of surfing Darwinism, Sebastian Inlet is one of the first places that gets mentioned.

Out on the north jetty, the competition among fishermen is a little less fierce, but it's still one of the premier fishing locations of Brevard County. Redfish, snook, bluefish, sharks, and tarpon are all regular catches. The bait and tackle shop at the inlet is a full-service place that sells everything you need, including rods, reels, and lures. A catwalk runs out into the inlet underneath the bridge—a popular shrimping area at the right time of year.

The gazebo on the north side of Sebastian Inlet State Park.

A long boardwalk runs above the sea oats out to the beach, with a nice gazebo along the way to stop and watch the waves from the shade. The beach is roomy, and extends well over a mile to the north without any development. Lifeguards patrol the beach by the inlet during summer months.

Up the road at the Inlet Marina, charter boats run fishermen out into the Atlantic, kayaks, canoes, and powerboats are available for rental, and eco-tours go down the river on a forty-nine-passenger boat to visit the Pelican Island National Wildlife Refuge. This was the first designated national wildlife refuge in the United States, and has a fabulous variety of bird life, especially in nesting season. A more recently designated refuge in this area is the Archie Carr National Wildlife Refuge, a discontinuous stretch of parcels over 20 miles from Wabasso Beach through Sebastian Inlet up to Melbourne. Archie Carr was a prominent turtle expert at the University of Florida, and the refuge is an attempt to preserve some of the most promising nesting areas for turtles along the coast.

ACCESS: From the north, take exit 71 off I–95 onto US 192 east. Follow this across the Melbourne Causeway to A1A, turn right onto A1A, and go 18 miles south to Sebastian Inlet.

From the south, exit I–95 onto Fellsmere Road east (SR 512). Within 5 miles look for CR 510 on your right. Follow 510 all the way to the coast and A1A, turn left onto A1A, and go 7 miles north to Sebastian Inlet.

PARKING: Huge lot, hundreds of spaces.

HOURS/FEES: Twenty-four hours; $3.25 per vehicle.

AMENITIES: Fishing jetty, bait and tackle shop, marina, kayak rentals, food concession, covered pavilions, rest rooms, showers, lifeguards, picnic areas.

ACTIVITIES: Surfing, fishing, sunbathing, river tours, kayaking, picnicking.

FOR MORE INFORMATION: Sebastian Inlet State Park (321) 984–4852.

Pelican Island National Wildlife Refuge (800) 952–1126.

Inlet Marina (321) 724–5424.

Sebastian Inlet State Park, South Side

The beach is the great attraction of the park on the south side of Sebastian Inlet. Nearly 2 miles of beautiful beach extends south of the inlet all the way down to the McLarty Treasure Museum. Because the dunes aren't as steep as farther south, the beaches don't suffer as badly from erosion. Reefs near shore break down the swell substantially before it reaches the beach. Also located in this portion is a boat ramp, a dock, rest rooms, and a fishing museum.

Fishing is possible off the south jetty and all along the beach, and Sebastian is known for some of the best inlet fishing in the state (though the north jetty is far more popular for this). A spooky surf break called Monster Hole sits far offshore of the south jetty, which breaks when huge north swells push down the coast. This break is a *long* paddle out from the beach, more than a third of a mile, and the waves unload on a shallow sandbar formed by the inlet currents. When the conditions are right, the waves peel perfectly for more than 100 yards.

At the south end of the beach is the McLarty Treasure Museum, situated where in 1715 a hurricane wrecked a treasure fleet returning to Spain. The museum was built at the site of the survivors' camp, and houses treasure and salvaged bits from the fleet along with history of the shipwreck. There is a separate admission fee from the rest of the park, though parking is free.

ACCESS: From the north, take exit 71 off I–95 southbound onto US 192 east. Follow this across the Melbourne Causeway to A1A, turn right onto A1A, and proceed 18 miles to Sebastian Inlet.

From the south, exit I–95 northbound onto Fellsmere Road east (SR 512). Within 5 miles look for CR 510 on your right. Follow 510 all the way to the coast and A1A, turn left onto A1A, and go 7 miles to Sebastian Inlet.

PARKING: There is a beachside parking area with rest rooms and showers 0.5 mile south of the jetty, as well as a small parking area at the treasure museum. There is substantial parking by the south jetty, which is accessed through the south-side entrance gate.

HOURS/FEES: The park is open twenty-four hours. The entrance fee is $3.25, though day use of the beachside parking is free. McLarty Treasure Museum is open 10:00 A.M.–4:30 P.M.

AMENITIES: Showers, rest rooms, dock, boat ramp, fishing jetty, camping.

ACTIVITIES: Surfing, fishing, kayaking, beach walking, picnicking, scuba diving.

FOR MORE INFORMATION: Sebastian Inlet State Park (321) 984–4852.

Jaycee Park

Just north of Beachland Boulevard on either A1A or Ocean Drive, the park occupies 8.3 acres, with a quarter-mile-long boardwalk extending to the south. The boardwalk has benches every few yards and a number of different walkways down to the beach. Overlooking the beach in the middle of the park is the Seaside Grill, which has daily meal specials and serves Edy's Ice Cream. Much of the parkland is taken up by an extensive grassy area with picnic pavilions and a children's playground. It's the largest and most popular picnic location in the city, and it's very well maintained.

Though the seas can easily get rough enough to be dangerous, most of Indian River County gets less surf than elsewhere, and thus the swimming conditions are generally better. The reason for the lack of surf is offshore reefs; diving is possible, though not spectacular. The reefs off Tracking Station Park to the north of Jaycee are probably more popular for this, and they're not comparable to the reefs of the south end of the Treasure Coast.

ACCESS: From I–95, take exit 68 onto SR 60 east and follow it across US 1 and the Merrill Barber Bridge to A1A. Turn left and go 0.75 mile north until you see Jaycee Park on your right.

PARKING: Approximately 150 spaces, but they fill up quickly due to the lack of other facilities.

HOURS/FEES: Sunrise–sunset; free.

AMENITIES: Showers, rest rooms, lifeguards, phones; Bethel Creek House conference center is available for rent.

ACTIVITIES: Swimming, surfing, picnicking, diving.

FOR MORE INFORMATION: Jaycee Park (772) 231–0578.

South Beach Park

South Beach Park has a lush grassy area with picnic pavilions, outdoor grills, rest rooms, and showers. Coming back to your car on hot summer days, when the sand has flame-broiled your feet by the time you reach the boardwalk, it's nice to cross over to a little oasis like this where you can shower, cool off, and relax before the ride home.

The beach is one of the widest ones along the northern Treasure Coast, allowing for volleyball courts on the oceanfront and plenty of room for people to spread out. Because Vero Beach has been known for years as a second-home or retirement community, it's been a pretty quiet place for young people. The advantage to having limited possibilities for going to the beach is that places like South Beach Park are a bustling mix of young, old, and families. It's a pretty happening scene for a town that's known primarily for being the spring training home of the Los Angeles Dodgers. And there's miles of unguarded beach to go traipsing off on to the south.

Vero Beach.

ACCESS: From I–95, take exit 68 onto SR 60 east and turn right onto US 1. Go for 0.5 mile to 17th Street, turn left, and follow the 17th Street Causeway across until it dead-ends at the beach.

PARKING: There are 170 parking spaces at South Beach Park, which can go pretty quickly.

HOURS/FEES: Sunrise–sunset; free.

AMENITIES: Showers, rest rooms, lifeguards, phones.

ACTIVITIES: Swimming, volleyball, surfing, picnicking, beach walking, diving.

FOR MORE INFORMATION: South Beach Park (772) 231–4700.

Avalon

The state government has a habit of quietly buying up large chunks of land with poor development value and making them just as quietly available to the public. Avalon Beach is such a place, part of a 570-acre parcel on North Hutchinson Island that adds yet more variety to the great beach opportunities in this area of Fort Pierce. There isn't much at Avalon but empty beach, which suits those seeking sun and seclusion.

A couple of small parking lots and walkovers give access to the beach, and rest rooms are provided. Fishing is popular, with fewer people in the water to conflict with than elsewhere. signs warn swimmers to be careful of underwater obstructions, because the navy built underwater obstacle courses of concrete and steel to train their frogmen teams. Most of this debris is deeply buried under sand now, but without lifeguards it pays to be careful.

Across the road just to the south is the Jack Island Preserve, a state facility on the Indian River. Jack Island has a variety of hiking trails and makes a fantastic place for bird-watching and photography.

ACCESS: From the north, 1–95 southbound, take exit 67 east onto Indrio Road and go to US 1. Continue right on US 1 for about 3 miles to North A1A, turn left, and go across the causeway out to the coast. Turn left at the stoplight to follow A1A north and the park will be on your right within 2 miles.

From the south, I–95 northbound, take exit 66 east onto Orange Avenue (SR 68) and go to US 1; continue left on US 1 about 2 miles to North A1A, turn right, and go across the causeway out to the coast. From there, see above directions.

PARKING: Two small lots of thirty spaces each.

HOURS/FEES: 8:00 A.M.–sunset; free.

AMENITIES: Rest rooms.

ACTIVITIES: Fishing, beachcombing, sun worship.

FOR MORE INFORMATION: Fort Pierce Inlet State Park (772) 468–3985.

Pepper Beach County Park

This is one of the few major public beaches with lifeguards for a long while along North Hutchinson Island. Recognizing this fact, the county has upgraded it over the years from a dirt turnoff among the pines to a huge, modern park with something for everyone. There are volleyball, tennis, and basketball courts, and the park extends from the beach all the way to the Indian River, where there are fishing docks and boat slips.

Covering 2,000 feet in length, there's plenty of room at this beach. Just to the south are the Fort Pierce Inlet state lands, and to the north you'll find more state-owned beach to explore. The beach slopes gently to the water like its neighbors, and is a good place to splash around near shore with little fear of rip currents or undertows.

ACCESS: From the north, I–95 southbound, exit east onto Indrio Road and go to US 1. Turn right onto US 1 and drive about 3 miles to North A1A; turn left and go across the causeway out to the coast. Turn left at the stoplight to follow A1A north, and the park will be on your right within a mile.

From the south, I–95 northbound, exit east onto Orange Avenue (SR 68) and go to US 1. Turn left onto US 1 and drive about 2 miles to North A1A; turn right and go across the causeway out to the coast. From there see directions above.

PARKING: Large parking area.

HOURS/FEES: Sunrise–sunset; free.

AMENITIES: Lifeguards, volleyball courts, tennis courts, basketball courts, rest rooms, showers, picnic tables, grills, fishing docks.

ACTIVITIES: Swimming, bodysurfing, volleyball, basketball, tennis, fishing.

FOR MORE INFORMATION: St. Lucie County Parks (772) 462–1521.

Fort Pierce Inlet State Park

Typical of a state facility, the north side of Fort Pierce Inlet is far more than just a beach. There are nature trails through coastal hammock, youth camp facilities, and picnic areas throughout the 340-acre park. Popular with surfers, the waves near the long north jetty are protected from strong southerly winds. An older crew of surfers tends to frequent the place, and longboards are more common here.

On the Indian River side of the recreation area, stands of red mangrove border a region called Dynamite Point. There isn't much in the way of access to this part of the park except by wading or canoe, but there is a picnic area in this corner.

The half-mile-long stretch that forms the ocean beach is reached by a long boardwalk through sea oats and beach grasses to a fairly expansive, white-sand beach. Its blessed by an abundance of natural sand due to the southerly flow of sand along the coast, which gets trapped by the north jetties of inlets. The slope of the bottom going out into the ocean is very gentle, so its an excellent place for swimming. Waves dissipate their energy a long way out from the beach, and the area near shore is shallow enough for children to wade around in. One place to be careful is up against the jetty, where a rip current can drag swimmers out to sea.

ACCESS: From the north, I–95 southbound, take exit 67 east onto Indrio Road and go to US 1. Turn right onto US 1 and continue about 3 miles to North A1A. Turn left, go across the causeway out to the coast, and Fort Pierce Inlet State Park will be on your right.

From the south, I–95 northbound, take exit 66 east onto Orange Avenue (SR 68) and go to US 1. Turn left onto US 1 and continue

The jetty at Fort Pierce Inlet State Park.

about 2 miles to North A1A; turn right and go across the causeway out to the coast. Fort Pierce Inlet State Park will be on your right.

PARKING: Large parking area.

HOURS/FEES: 8:00 A.M.–sunset; $3.25 per vehicle.

AMENITIES: Showers, rest rooms, picnic areas, youth camp, summer lifeguards, trails.

ACTIVITIES: Swimming, surfing, picnicking, hiking, bird-watching.

FOR MORE INFORMATION: Fort Pierce Inlet State Park (772) 468–3985.

Beach Walk

(Written by Jane Wood Reno, the author's grandmother, 1966.)

For six days I walked 104 miles up the beaches of the Florida east coast, from Jupiter Light to Patrick Air Force Base. Two nights I slept on the beach, walking on between naps.

In a bag slung on one shoulder I carried cheese, raisins, and bell peppers, water in a plastic one-pint detergent bottle, a bug bomb, a very light water-repellent jacket with hood, a plastic bag to keep my legs warm, plenty of matches, cigarettes, comb, Kleenex, a map, lipstick, and enough money.

After noting on the first day that I could skinny-dip in complete privacy almost anywhere along that beach, I left my bathing suit behind to lighten the load and had no cause to regret it until the last day, when I reached a populated beach. The idea that walking up the beach would be a good vacation came to me after the phone had rung incessantly all one day and into the evening. After studying the map, I picked that stretch because it seemed the least populated on Florida's east coast. Unpopulated it proved to be, for many, many miles.

I knew that Jonathan Dickinson, his wife, baby, and others had been shipwrecked along there in the eighteenth century and found it so desolate that a number of their party died before they finished their walk to St. Augustine. But they walked hungry, naked, in the winter, and were prisoners of hostile Indians.

I picked the first week in May, and on the nights I did not sleep on the beach, I called my daughter-in-law, Vera, who lives in Stuart. She came and picked me up, fed me a good dinner, and I slept comfortably in her house.

The thing I learned was faith.

Have faith that walking is a means of getting somewhere, and the blue headlands before you will fade into the blue distance behind you.

If, upon walking on the second day, you totter along the sand with new muscles in your legs and feet complaining, put one foot in front of the other for three minutes and the kinks and pains will go, and you can step out happily. The same thing holds true with a cramp in the calf of the leg in midafternoon.

Have faith that you can walk 20 miles on a pint of water, and you will find you can, especially if the water tastes slightly of detergent. This will deter you from wanting too much water.

The same dense, beautiful, and inpenetrable green that was so forbidding to Jonathan Dickinson mantles the rolling dune behind the beach today for many miles. Sea grapes, palmettos, and cocoplum are woven together into a wall. Only the shorebirds that were laying pink eggs, raccoons, and a little animal that left tiny tracks and wedge-shaped holes in the sand seemed to find the underbrush hospitable.

The little tracks proved to be those of armadillos; they like to stick their noses in the sand now and then. There were no signs of the small bears that used to come down to Jupiter Beach to eat turtle eggs when Captain Bill Gray and his brother, Herman, camped out there in 1909.

That coast is fringed by long, narrow islands, and it was on the beaches of those islands I walked. There is no bridge across the St. Lucie Inlet at the northern tip of Jupiter Island, the first stretch of my journey. I should have had to backtrack 8 miles or so had a fisherman not ferried me across that inlet to the southern tip of Hutchinson Island.

To me the Stuart House of Refuge, about 2 miles north of St. Lucie's inlet, was just that: Built in the 1880s to afford succor to shipwrecked sailors who might otherwise have perished from hunger and thirst on that desolate coast, it is today maintained as a fascinating little museum by the local historical society, and I rested there luxuriously. Just off shore treasure hunters were working.

A road is being built the length of Hutchinson Island, but it is not yet completed, and access to the beach for many miles north of Jensen's Beach is only possible by foot or by beach buggy. That shimmering, firm, level strand was populated mostly by birds. There is no bridge across Fort Pierce Inlet, at the northern tip of this island, and I went back to the mainland there across the Fort Pierce causeway.

The third island, which I was told is also called Hutchinson Island, is about 30 miles long. My map showed no road north of Wabasso Beach, and no bridge over Sebastian Inlet. Just at dawn I rounded the northern tip of that island, and there was the most beautiful new bridge arching over Sebastian Inlet. Later I found it was opened in February. That was when I really pondered on the message: Have faith.

For six days I walked when I wanted to walk, ate when I wanted to eat, and slept when and where I wanted to sleep. In the nights when I got sleepy, I combed the eroding sandy bluff to a casuarina tree, scraped up some needles and small dead twigs and branches, and started a little fire.

After my feet were warm, I put out the fire and raked the hot sand out to make a bed. My bag was my pillow, and I wiggled out curves in the sand to fit. Never did I have a sounder, sweeter sleep—even though I usually waked chilly in two or three hours. The chill went away when I walked. The nights were most magical after the moon had set, for the stars were higher and so lavish in their brightness that I could see the white crests of all the curling waves.

At the end, I backtracked, and my walk ended in a little white board building overlooking a splendid beach opposite Melbourne Beach trailer village. The sign says simply, THE BAR. For six days I had talked to almost no strangers. I plodded in and over my beer visited with the bartenders, Janie and Jamie.

I told them what I had been doing. Jamie came from behind the bar and put soothing drops in my eyes and rubbed my ankles. Bob Jacobs, a customer, sent across the street to the trailer village for an electric vibrating machine, unplugged the jukebox, and massaged my legs. Nobody would let me buy a beer.

So . . . it might be that someday I shall be drowned by the sea, or die of pneumonia from sleeping out at night, or be robbed and strangled by strangers. These things happen. Even so, I shall be ahead because of trusting the beach, the night, and strangers . . .

Footprints in the sand.

Region 5

Although in the shadow of the Bahamas at its lower end, the Treasure Coast is still open to a great range of the Atlantic Ocean's power. For wave aficionados this is a boon, with surf spots here providing some of the best waves in Florida. The force of the seas has also been the curse of some, from the unfortunate Jonathan Dickinson to Spanish treasure fleets to modern-day coast dwellers whose homes are in constant danger of being washed away by northeasters and hurricanes.

After reaching the south side of Fort Pierce Inlet on A1A, you'll find a group of public beaches that add up more than a mile in length, including South Jetty Park, South Beach Park, Surfside Park, and a variety of dune walkovers. At times the south jetty beaches have been nice, but they have suffered so badly from severe erosion that they are not covered in this guide. Condos sprout up and quickly disappear again, taking you into a 10-mile stretch of undeveloped coast where you can go horseback riding at the beach. Farther along is the St. Lucie nuclear power plant. On either side of the plant are the fine fishing and surf beaches of Turtle Creek and Walton Rocks. The ocean is teeming with life around the warm-water outflow, and some large and scary sea creatures normally only found in deep water hang around here.

Condos erupt again for the remainder of the county length, before crossing into Martin County, which is noticeably different due to a four-story height limit on buildings. Jensen Beach and Stuart Beach are the main public beaches, with a wealth of other free, twenty-four-hour-access parking areas between and beyond. Where the road dead-ends at the bottom of the island is the beautiful snorkeling area, Bathtub Reef Beach.

A1A takes a long detour from the coast between Stuart and Hobe Sound, missing one of the best beaches in Florida. The entire 5.5 miles of the north end of Jupiter Island is roadless wilderness, combining the St. Lucie Inlet State Preserve and the Hobe Sound National Wildlife Refuge. The inlet park includes the waters 1.5 miles out to sea, which contain the best shallow reef diving in the area. Resuming at Hobe Sound Public Beach, A1A meanders south through the town of Jupiter Island, the wealthiest community in the United States.

Toward the bottom of the island, geysers blast through the coquina rock holes at Blowing Rocks, then give way to the gentle sands of Coral Cove Beach. The Loxahatchee River empties out at the Jupiter Inlet, a river important in Seminole Indian legend. Up in the narrow headwaters, the river twists through a gorgeous cypress canopy and is designated as one of the National Wild and Scenic Rivers of the country. Historians still argue whether the river's name originally meant "white man lied" about an offered truce during the Seminole Wars, or whether it translates to the more innocuous "turtle" river.

Access

I–95, US 1, and A1A are the main north–south arteries. A1A is the road of choice to use over this section because I–95 is well away from the coast and US 1 is congested.

From the south, take I–95 to the Hobe Sound exit and go east on Bridge Road out to A1A.

From the north, take I–95 to the Fellsmere exit, go east to CR 510, and follow it to A1A.

Beaches

- Frederick Douglass Beach
- Walton Rocks Beach/Turtle Creek Beach
- Jensen Public Beach aka Sea Turtle Beach
- Stuart Beach
- Bathtub Reef Beach
- St. Lucie Inlet State Preserve
- Hobe Sound National Wildlife Refuge
- Hobe Sound Public Beach
- Blowing Rocks Preserve
- Coral Cove Beach

Camping

Savannas Recreation Area—(772) 464–7855, (800) 789–5776. Located 6.2 miles east of I–95 on Midway Road in Port St. Lucie. There are three types of campsites for general use, from water only to water/electric to water/electric/sewage. Hot and cold showers, water fill-up station, laundry facilities, public telephones, on-site utilities, boat ramp (7.5-horsepower max). MasterCard and Visa accepted.

Jonathan Dickinson State Park—Reservations (772) 546–2771. Between Hobe Sound and Jupiter on US 1, 135 campsites in a massive pineland park through which the Loxahatchee River flows. Fees are $14 from May through November and $16 from December through April.

Other Points of Interest

Elliott Museum—(772) 225–1961, at Stuart Beach. A tribute to automotive inventors Sterling and Harmon Elliott, this is an amazing collection of early-1900s automobiles, Americana, furniture, and Martin County history.

Florida Oceanographic Society—(772) 225–0505, at Stuart Beach. Reef exhibits, saltwater tanks, information on Bathtub Reef and other area reefs.

New York Mets Spring Training—(772) 871–5476, between St. Lucie West Boulevard and Midway Road, just east of I–95. Catch the Mets during spring training or watch a minor-league game.

Gilbert's Bar House of Refuge—(772) 225–1875, between Stuart Beach and Bathtub Reef. Built in 1875 as a haven for shipwrecked sailors, it is the only remaining House of Refuge in existence. During World War II it was used as a lookout post to spot German submarines that were wreaking havoc with shipping just off the coast. Open daily 10:00 A.M.–4:00 P.M. The fee is $4.00 for adults, $2.00 for children ages six through thirteen; under six free.

Hobe Sound Nature Center—(772) 546–2067, on US 1 south of Bridge Road. Displays—and sometimes handling—of local snakes, baby crocodiles and alligators. Also turtle walks at the wildlife refuge beach.

Jupiter Lighthouse—(561) 747–8380. This ancient lighthouse was built in 1860 and has recently benefited from restoration work. Visible from the US 1 bridge over Jupiter Inlet. Open for climbing Sunday through Wednesday, 10:00 A.M.–3:15 P.M.; $5.00.

Region 5

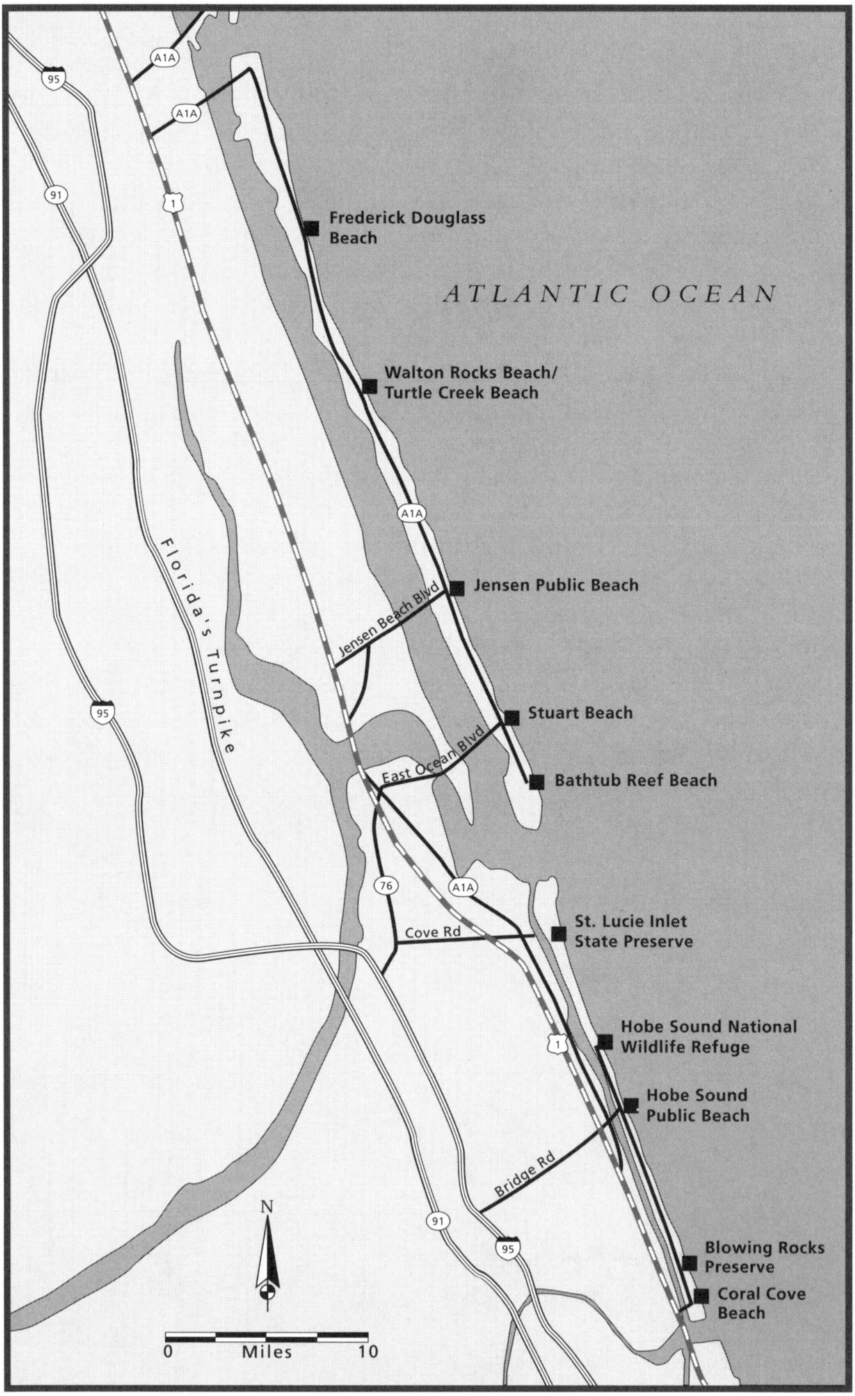
A1A
95
1
91
Frederick Douglass Beach
ATLANTIC OCEAN
Walton Rocks Beach/ Turtle Creek Beach
Florida's Turnpike
Jensen Public Beach
Jensen Beach Blvd
Stuart Beach
East Ocean Blvd
Bathtub Reef Beach
76
Cove Rd
St. Lucie Inlet State Preserve
Hobe Sound National Wildlife Refuge
Hobe Sound Public Beach
Bridge Rd
N
Blowing Rocks Preserve
Coral Cove Beach
0
Miles
10

Frederick Douglass Beach

Four miles south of Fort Pierce Inlet, this secluded beach is in the northern half of a wonderfully empty 10-mile strip of southern St. Lucie County. The nuclear power plant is partly to thank for this quietness, since having one in your backyard has not historically been a great selling point for developers. In addition, property owners can't get public water. The beachgoing public is the lucky beneficiary, and around Frederick Douglass the coast is empty for miles in either direction. It is the only public beach on the whole Treasure Coast that promotes horseback riding on the beach, and horse owners from the western part of Martin and St. Lucie Counties take advantage of it. Lifeguards patrol the beach during summer months, which is the only part of the year the beach sees much use. During winter months it's a quiet oasis for beach strollers and surf fishermen.

ACCESS: From the north, I–95 southbound, exit east onto Orange Avenue (SR 68) to US 1; go left on US 1 approximately 1.5 miles to South A1A. Turn right, cross the causeway, and follow A1A south 4 miles.

From the south, the park is 12 miles north of Jensen Beach on A1A.

PARKING: Large dirt parking area.

HOURS/FEES: Sunrise–sunset; free.

AMENITIES: Summer lifeguards, rest rooms, wheelchair-accessible boardwalk, showers, picnic tables.

ACTIVITIES: Horseback riding, sunbathing, swimming, surfing, fishing.

FOR MORE INFORMATION: St. Lucie County Parks (772) 462–1521.

Walton Rocks Beach/Turtle Creek Beach

There are many nice beach access points in St. Lucie County in the surprisingly uninhabited stretch of coast between the northern condos of the south county strip and the southern condos of Fort Pierce, but only one separates itself as being a bit more special than the rest. This is Walton Rocks Beach, a short distance to the south of the Florida Power and Light nuclear plant's water intake and outlet pipes.

One of the things that differentiates it is that it's one of the few beaches along here with a rest room, but it's also a wider beach than most. You access it down a hard shell road through fields of mangroves that eventually opens up into a large, unpaved parking area. A short boardwalk leads to the beach, and a patchy reef lies in shallow water less than 100 yards offshore. A diver got sucked into the intake pipe over a decade ago and spit into the intake canal, scraped up but relatively unharmed.

When nowhere else on Hutchinson Island has surf big enough to ride, Walton Rocks often does. Whether this has to do with the reef, the shallow-water shoals 4 miles offshore, or the mysteries of nuclear power, who knows. The beach is also popular with fishermen, because the warm water emanating from the power plant makes the area unusually abundant with sea life.

On the north side of the plant, just after crossing the intake canal, there is another shell road with a TURTLE CREEK NATURE TRAIL sign. This takes you to a very small parking area on the beach, with the entrance to the mile-long nature trail at the south end. The trail starts off sandy, switches to boardwalk, and is covered with wood chips in sections. It's closed Monday, Saturday, and holidays, and though it's self-guided, the signs claim you have to check in at FPL's Energy Encounter building.

ACCESS: From the north, I–95 southbound, exit east onto Orange Avenue (SR 68) to US 1. Go left on US 1 approximately 1.5 miles to South A1A, turn right, cross the causeway, and follow A1A south for 8 miles. Turtle Creek Beach is just before the power plant, and Walton Rocks Beach is on the south side of the power plant.

From the south, the park is 8 miles north of Jensen Beach on A1A.

PARKING: Large dirt parking area.

HOURS/FEES: Sunrise–sunset; free.

Opposite page: Lifeguard on duty.

AMENITIES: Rest rooms, boardwalk, showers, picnic tables.

ACTIVITIES: Surfing, fishing, diving, hiking, nature viewing, glowing.

FOR MORE INFORMATION: St. Lucie County Parks (772) 462–1521.

Florida Power and Light Energy Encounter (772) 468–4111.

Jensen Public Beach aka Sea Turtle Beach

Sea Turtle Beach, known to locals as Jensen Public Beach, is the biggest public beach facility in Martin County. There is parking available for approximately 400 cars, along with showers, rest rooms, picnic areas, phones, volleyball courts, and lifeguards. Formerly a run-of-the-mill public beach with sprawling dirt parking areas, the facility got a makeover about ten years ago. New land was added, greatly extending the beachfront, and all the conveniences were modernized including the paving of most of the parking lot. Now it's the best major public beach in the county. The nicest feature is the large deck overlooking the ocean, with many umbrella-covered tables and a concession that sells a wide variety of food.

Situated where the Jensen Beach Causeway meets A1A, it's easily accessible from the mainland. If you're online, log on to www.martin.fl.us/beachcam.html, which features a beachcam shot from the neighboring Holiday Inn, updated hourly. Shops are located within walking distance on A1A, including pizza and sandwich places, a bank, and a convenience store. A large surf shop nearby carries just about everything you could want for the beach. The actual town of Jensen Beach is located on the mainland side, so if there's anything you can't get out at the beach, you can likely get it with a short drive over the causeway.

ACCESS: From the north, I–95 southbound, exit onto Midway Road east and go to US 1. Turn right onto US 1 and go to Jensen Beach Boulevard, then turn left onto Jensen Beach Boulevard until it deadends at Indian River Drive. Turn left and proceed a few hundred yards to the Jensen Beach Causeway; turn right and follow it to the beach.

From the south, I–95 northbound, exit SR 76 east and go to US 1. Turn left onto US 1 and cross the Roosevelt Bridge. Turn right at the first light, then left at the next light onto Savannah Road, and go to Jensen Beach Boulevard. Turn right and follow this road until it dead-ends at Indian River Drive; turn left and proceed a few hundred yards to the Jensen Beach Causeway. Turn right and follow it to the beach.

From the Florida Turnpike—exit east at Port St. Lucie Boulevard to US 1. Turn right onto US 1 and go to Jensen Beach Boulevard; from there, see the directions above.

PARKING: Four hundred spaces.

HOURS/FEES: Twenty-four hours; free.

AMENITIES: Food concession, deck with covered tables, showers, rest rooms, lifeguards, picnic area, grills, volleyball courts.

ACTIVITIES: Swimming, volleyball, surfing, sunbathing.

FOR MORE INFORMATION: Martin County Parks (772) 221–1418.

Sunrise Surf Shop wave report (772) 229–1723.

Beachcam www.co.martin.fl.us/beachcam.html.

Stuart Beach

One of the most popular of the Martin County beaches, Stuart Beach has a lot to offer. Encompassing eight acres of beachfront, there is plenty of room to spread out between the north and south ends. There are two different lifeguard towers, so if one is closed up it means the guards are down at the other end that day. Since Stuart is the only public beach with basketball courts, there are quite often feisty pickup games going on. Be warned, though: Some of these guys are merciless hackers.

A snack bar with an elevated deck and covered tables offers a place to get some shade and refreshment, and picnic shelters are strewn throughout the park as well. Next door is the Elliott Museum, which houses a remarkable collection of 1890–1920 automobiles. If you're a vintage-car buff, don't miss it. The Elliott also has a good Martin County history section, and special displays that come and go. On the opposite side of A1A is the Florida Oceanographic Society, with saltwater tanks and a lot of information on area reefs.

A short walk to the north of Stuart Beach is the Tiger Shores Beach Access; to the south is Fletcher Beach, where exposed formations of coquina rock erupt from the sand. These rock formations continue down through the

House of Refuge and on to Bathtub Reef Beach. The House of Refuge is the oldest structure in Martin County, built in 1875 as a haven for shipwrecked sailors, and the only remaining example of these rescue stations along the Florida coast. Just 100 yards off the House of Refuge is a wreck in about 15 feet of water that's fun to dive.

ACCESS: From I–95, take exit 61 and go east on SR 76 to the fourth light—Monterey Road. Turn right onto Monterey Road (stay left at the fork) and follow it to the end, crossing US 1 and A1A. Turn right onto East Ocean Boulevard and go over two drawbridges. Just after A1A curves to the north, you will pass the Elliott Museum; Stuart Beach is on your right.

PARKING: Two hundred-plus spaces.

HOURS/FEES: Twenty-four hours; free.

AMENITIES: Showers, rest rooms, lifeguards, picnic area, basketball courts, food concession, deck with covered tables.

ACTIVITIES: Swimming, basketball, surfing, sunbathing.

FOR MORE INFORMATION: Martin County Parks (772) 221–1418.

Florida Oceanographic Society (772) 225–0505.

Gilbert's Bar House of Refuge (772) 225–1875.

Elliott Museum (772) 225–1961.

Bathtub Reef Beach

If you find yourself at Bathtub Reef Beach and someone tells you to be on the lookout for "hairy blennies and puddingwives," don't be alarmed. While further suggestions about the wealth of beaugregories (a Cajun putdown?) may leave you baffled, you may think yourself finally on familiar ground when the rock hind is mentioned. Everyone appreciates a good rock hind, you acknowledge with a wink. In fact, all of the above are tropical reef fish that you're likely to see while snorkeling in the shallow waters of Bathtub Reef.

The reef starts at the north end of the beach, where the coast juts out a bit, and runs roughly parallel to the beach for a mile all the way down to the St. Lucie Inlet. The sheltered pocket at the north end is known as Bathtub Reef, or The Bathtub. Long a favorite of locals, it has become more widely

Underwater life.

known to outsiders in recent years as a great family play spot. When the ocean is rough, this is always a protected place to go for a swim.

The popularity of the public beach comes from its uniqueness. There are few other places in Florida where you can enjoy this abundance of marine life within 100 feet of the beach. Rather than the colorful coral of the Florida Keys, the reef is made up of wormrock, created by years and years of building by the *Sabellariid* worm. It is easily damaged, and you are forced to walk over it when it is completely exposed at low tide, so take care in your journey through it. Aside from the really odd-sounding fish, the reef has damselfish, parrotfish, blue crabs, snapper, triggerfish, Atlantic guitarfish, grouper, snook, scorpionfish, angelfish, sheepshead, sea urchins, and much more. There are deeper reefs not far outside the shallow one, and it's possible to spend all day exploring the caves and ledges there.

If you walk south from The Bathtub, you can wander all the way down to the north jetty of the St. Lucie Inlet, then along more beach and sandbars just inside the inlet. The residents of Sailfish Point don't seem to use the beaches much, so take advantage of the emptiness. It effectively extends the beach for a couple more miles. Hardly more than 100 yards to the north is another public beach, Chastain Beach, which is extremely popular with surfers. A homeowner in between has put up illegal signs in the water and on the beach warning people not to trespass, but pay them no attention. Not only is it public domain below the mean high-tide line, but the public is allowed right of passage between the dune vegetation and the water throughout Florida. The nearest store to buy food and drink is all the way back on the other side of Indian River Plantation 5 miles away, so make sure you stock a cooler before coming out.

ACCESS: From I–95, take exit 61 and go east on SR 76 to the fourth light—Monterey Road. Go right onto Monterey Road (stay left at a fork) to its end. Go right onto East Ocean Boulevard (over two drawbridges) to MacArthur Boulevard (traffic light). Go right through Indian River Plantation and follow the road all the way to the end, just before the gates of the private Sailfish Point community.

PARKING: You'll find 160 spaces.

HOURS/FEES: Twenty-four hours; free.

AMENITIES: Rest rooms, showers, picnic tables, lifeguards.

ACTIVITIES: Snorkeling, swimming, scuba diving, beach walking, fishing.

FOR MORE INFORMATION: Martin County Parks (772) 221–1418.

Florida Oceanographic Society (772) 225–0505.

St. Lucie Inlet State Preserve

At the northern end of Jupiter Island, miles of empty beach beyond the last house, the St. Lucie Inlet State Preserve occupies 928 pristine acres of Florida coastal wilderness. Bordered at the northern end by the St. Lucie Inlet and the Hobe Sound National Wildlife Refuge to the south, the preserve is an undeveloped section of barrier island with a maze of mangrove creeks that lead from the Intracoastal Waterway out to the empty beach. Less than a half mile offshore, shallow reefs are also encompassed within the preserve's boundaries. These reefs are popular in the area with snorkelers and scuba divers, and as a result the preserve actually gets far more underwater use than land use. Completing it all, 3 quiet miles of sandy beach await those who value serenity.

The back creeks, which are becoming increasingly popular with kayakers, are really the best way to get to the beach. They trace the route of the old Jupiter Narrows, which was the waterway steamships plied before canals were dug to form the Intracoastal. There is also a 3,300-foot-long boardwalk

Beach walking at St. Lucie Inlet State Preserve.

that runs from the Intracoastal to the beach, allowing people with boats to dock on the river and see a cross section of the island. You can launch a canoe, kayak, or surfboard from the mainland to paddle the 200 yards across the river to the boardwalk.

The boardwalk crosses stands of mangroves and two coastal hammocks, full of live oak, cabbage palm, sea grapes, and other native plants and trees. Then there's miles of empty beach to play with. And what a beach! It's amazing how many days of the year you can walk the beach all alone out there, with no company but the wind sweeping through the sea oats. You never know what you'll find washed ashore either, from drug smugglers' boats to Cuban rafts. Turtles frequent the beach during nesting season, their nests often pillaged by raccoons or the occasional bobcat.

The swimming conditions vary widely, depending on the season. In summer the water is usually calm and relatively clear. During other times of year, the conditions are almost impossible to predict. The reef offshore breaks up the swell, though, so it is rarely ever too rough to swim. It's a marvel that the facilities are so high quality while the setting is so remote, but that's part of the charm of it all. There's good fishing off the south jetty of the St. Lucie Inlet, and some more picnic tables tucked back behind the dunes near it. The land still seems as it might have been when Jonathan Dickinson traipsed along it.

ACCESS: From I–95, head east at exit 61 onto SR 76. At the first light, turn right onto Cove Road. Stay on Cove Road for 6 miles until it dead-ends at the Intracoastal Waterway. The boardwalk/dock is on other side of the river.

PARKING: Small parking area at end of Cove Road; thirty boat slips at the dock.

HOURS/FEES: 8:00 A.M.–sunset; $2.00 per boat.

AMENITIES: Rest rooms, showers (when there's water), picnic pavilion, boardwalk, dock.

ACTIVITIES: Fishing, beach walking, diving, kayaking, nature viewing, bird-watching.

FOR MORE INFORMATION: St. Lucie Inlet State Preserve (772) 744–7603.

Hobe Sound National Wildlife Refuge

The Hobe Sound National Wildlife Refuge links together with the St. Lucie Inlet State Preserve to create some of the most beautiful 5.5 miles of undeveloped beach in all of Florida. The advantage to the refuge beach is that it's accessible by car, at the north end of the community of Jupiter Island. Many locals still know the beach at the parking area by the name North End, since it only became part of the refuge in the past decade.

The 735 acres of barrier island, extending 2 miles from the parking area to north of Peck's Lake, provides some of the most productive sea-turtle-nesting beach in the United States. Behind the beach and extending to the Intracoastal Waterway are acres of mangrove swamp, which used to extend beyond today's beach before erosion took its toll. The gnarled stumps and roots of black mangroves and, more recently, Australian pines are often found near the water line.

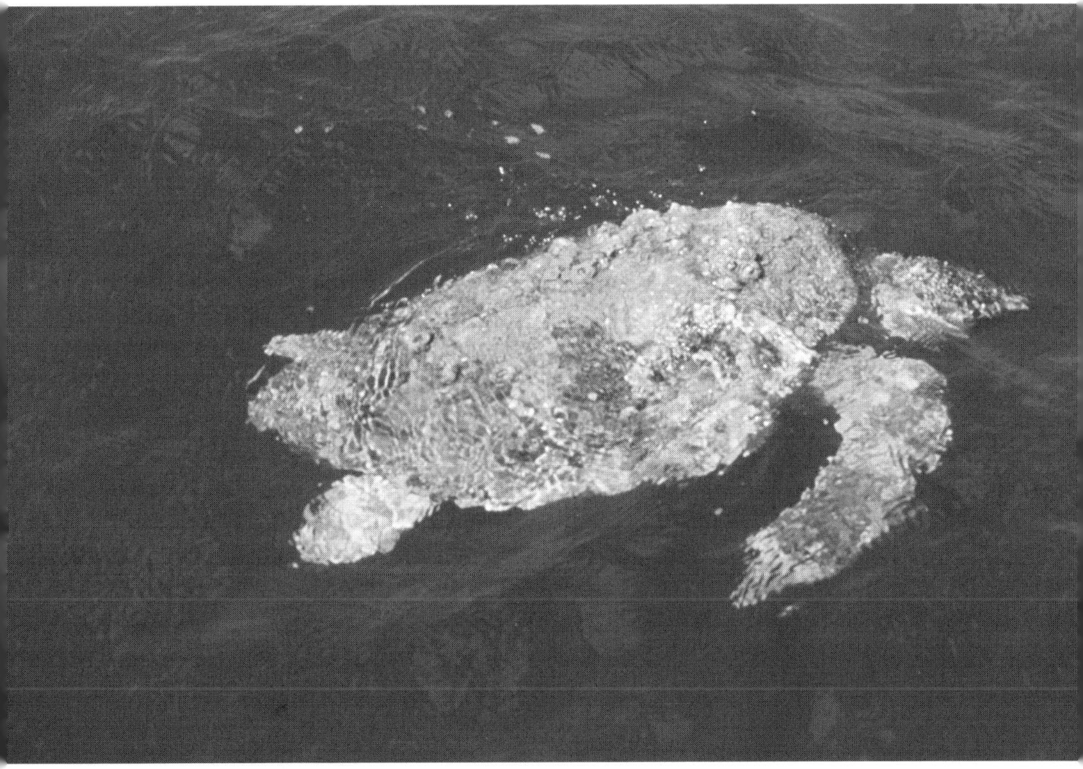

Sea turtle off Hobe Sound National Wildlife Refuge.

Toward the north end of the refuge is Peck's Lake, a popular beach for Intracoastal Waterway boaters. The barrier island narrows here to a thread no more than 50 yards wide, and the wide area of waterway between it and the mainland is Peck's Lake. A natural inlet broke through from the ocean in 1962–63, but was promptly filled in when it was discovered how quickly it was contributing to beach erosion to the south. Protected by offshore reefs, the surf at the Peck's Lake beach is usually quite gentle. The water gets deeper very gradually, so it's a great swimming spot.

The refuge beach more than a quarter mile north of the parking area has always been used by some as a nude beach. The main beach at the parking area has a couple of boardwalks across the dune, a changing shed, and portable toilets, but otherwise lacks amenities. This may not seem to justify the entrance fee, but it's the entirety of the refuge you're paying for. Since you pass by the Hobe Sound Public Beach on the way in and out, you can stop there to use the showers.

ACCESS: From I–95, take the Hobe Sound exit (exit 60) and follow Bridge Road east all the way to the coast. It empties into the Hobe Sound Public Beach, but turn left onto North Beach Road just before that. Follow this to the end, and you will come to the entry gate of the refuge.

PARKING: Eighty spaces.

HOURS/FEES: Sunrise–sunset; $5.00 per vehicle, $13.00 yearly pass, or free with Duck Stamp.

AMENITIES: Portable toilets, changing shed.

ACTIVITIES: Beachcombing, swimming, surfing, fishing, unofficial nude sunbathing.

FOR MORE INFORMATION: Hobe Sound National Wildlife Refuge (772) 546–6141; fax (772) 369–7190.

Hobe Sound Public Beach

One of Martin County's smaller guarded beaches, Hobe Sound Public makes up for what it lacks in size with some unique features. Having a free public access in the heart of Jupiter Island is almost remarkable in itself, since this community is the richest per-capita town in the United States, and the residents value their privacy. Unlike some other coastal communities of Florida, though, they don't begrudge people passing through. The residents, who have included a secretary of the interior under Nixon, a secretary of the treasury under Kennedy, and a former publisher of *Time* magazine, mostly come from genteel old money. The houses tend to sit so far back on densely landscaped lots that you often can't see them.

There's a large concrete pavilion and grassy area overlooking the beach, with plenty of tables under it and blessed shade. The beach is pretty wide, ironically as a result of severe erosion in the past. The dunes were washed away, only to have the beach eventually grow back wider than ever with the added space where the dunes had been. Only 100 feet off the beach is a very shallow wormrock reef popular for snorkeling. As long as there's no swell, the water is usually quite clear. Though the surf is often better at the refuge parking area up the road, this is one of the best spots on Jupiter Island when the waves get really big.

ACCESS: From I–95, take the Hobe Sound exit (exit 60) and follow Bridge Road east all the way to the coast. It empties into the beach parking.

PARKING: Eighty spaces.

HOURS/FEES: Twenty-four hours; free.

AMENITIES: Rest rooms, showers, pavilion, picnic tables, lifeguards.

ACTIVITIES: Snorkeling, swimming, fishing.

FOR MORE INFORMATION: Martin County Parks (772) 221–1418.

Blowing Rocks Preserve

Dividing the oceanfront condominiums of Palm Beach County from the exclusive luxury of the town of Jupiter Island is a small length of coastline that often escapes the attention of locals and visitors. It is Blowing Rocks Preserve, a seventy-three-acre tract owned by the Nature Conservancy. Home to the longest stretch of exposed Anastasia limestone on the Florida coastline, the name comes from the activity of surf pushing up through holes in the rock and blasting clouds of spray out the top. The Nature Conservancy has managed the coastal vegetation carefully, eliminating all the nonnative inhabitants like Australian pines to restore the flora balance to what it was like hundreds of years ago.

As you approach the path to the beach from the parking lot, a small information kiosk is nestled in the foliage. This is usually staffed by a volunteer, though it may not always be open. A sand path runs up to the beach, with a main trail branching off that leads through the dense mix of sea grape and palmetto to other dune crossings. Signs offer a wealth of information on the plant life as well as on the history of the rock structure.

In 1996 the Nature Conservancy added a new feature to the preserve, the $1.4 million Hawley Education Center. This Key West–style building houses classrooms and exhibits to teach people about the environment. One of the focuses of the center is the Indian River Lagoon, which extends from Jupiter Inlet north 156 miles to Ponce Inlet. A boardwalk runs out to the edge of the river, and there is also a native plant nursery. Around the center are interpretive areas of restored coastal strand, mangrove wetland, and tidal area, along with hardwood hammocks.

ACCESS: From exit 59 off I–95 or the Jupiter exit off the Florida Turnpike, take Indiantown Road east until you reach Alternate A1A. Turn left, and stay on it as it crosses two bridges and becomes North A1A on the beach. Blowing Rocks Preserve will appear after about 3 miles.

PARKING: Eighteen parking spaces.

HOURS/FEES: 6:00 A.M.–5:00 P.M.; $3.00 suggested donation.

AMENITIES: Boardwalk, trails, nature center, rest rooms, butterfly garden.

ACTIVITIES: Fishing, watching water shoot skyward, hiking, learning.

FOR MORE INFORMATION: Blowing Rocks Preserve (561) 744–6668.

Coral Cove Beach

Located at the south end of Jupiter Island, this is the only free public beach on the lower half of the island. There are 600 feet of ocean beach with year-round lifeguards, along with a similar 600 feet of frontage on the Intracoastal Waterway just across the road. You can river fish or surf fish within 100 yards of each other. For explorers, the north jetty of Jupiter Inlet is less than a mile to the south, and you can walk the beach all the way to the jetty.

The park has been considerably spruced up since the old days when it was just a sprawling dirt parking area laced with Australian pines, though it still maintains its old character. The stretch of A1A that runs from Coral Cove up to the Hobe Sound Public Beach is a favorite of bicyclists, and is a good way to mix a day at the beach with a peek at the lifestyles of the ultrarich and—unlike Palm Beach—discreet. Jupiter Island has always been a staid, old-money sort of community, and despite the celebrity of some newcomers like golfer Greg Norman, the island maintains a quiet, dignified pace.

Nearby is the Jupiter Lighthouse, a venerable structure well worth a visit. There are some great legends associated with it, including the time the lighthouse keeper kept hand cranking the light during one of the worst hurricanes to hit Florida in the twentieth century, the killer 1928 storm that Zora Neale Hurston wrote about in *Their Eyes Were Watching God.*

ACCESS: From exit 59 off I–95 or the Jupiter exit off the Florida Turnpike, take Indiantown Road east until you reach Alternate A1A. Turn left and stay on it as it crosses two bridges and becomes North A1A on the beach. Coral Cove will be on your right within a mile.

PARKING: There are 115 spaces.

HOURS/FEES: Sunrise–sunset; free.

AMENITIES: Picnic areas, grills, rest rooms, lifeguards, showers, nature area.

ACTIVITIES: Swimming, surfing, fishing.

FOR MORE INFORMATION: Beach conditions (561) 624–0065.

Palm Beach County Parks (561) 966–6600.

Jupiter Lighthouse (561) 747–8380.

The Shipwrecked Quaker

One of the first English accounts of the early Florida coastline came as a result of a ship's misfortune during the late seventeenth century. The barkentine *Reformation* was under sail from Jamaica to Philadelphia with five passengers on board, three of them being a Quaker named Jonathan Dickinson, his wife, and baby. Dickinson was later to become the mayor of Philadelphia. A September hurricane blew them ashore in 1696 near Jupiter Inlet, leaving them in "a wilderness country looking very dismal, having no trees, but only sand hills covered with shrubby palmetto."

After a pair of Indians came upon the passengers, captain, and dozen crew members, and threatened them with knives before taking some tobacco and running away, Dickinson wrote:

> We communed together and considered our condition, being amongst a barbarous people such as were generally accounted man-eaters.... We sat ourselves down, expecting cruelty and hard death....

The Indians returned with their chief and greater numbers and led Dickinson's party south to their settlement of Hoe-Bay at Jupiter Inlet (*jobe* in Spanish, mistaken alternately for *Jove* and *Hobe* by the English—hence the names for Jupiter and Hobe Sound). The shipwrecked group asked of the settlements of St. Lucia and St. Augustine to the north, but the Indians—who knew better—lied and insisted that those lay south. Finally the chief let them know St. Lucia was "about two or three days' journey thither and that when we came there, we should have our throats and scalps cut and be shot, burnt, and eaten."

After a few days at Hoe-Bay, the chief finally relented and let them take their leaky dinghy and proceed northward. The group encountered more Indians while paddling up the coast and were delayed at one village before making their way ashore on the south side of the St. Lucie Inlet. Immediately they were set upon again, and tormented by the easily amused Indians:

> And being all stripped as naked as we were born, and endeavoring to hide our nakedness; these cannibals took the books, and tearing out the leaves would give each of us a leaf to cover us; which we took from them: at which time they would deride and smite us;

> and instantly another of them would snatch away what the other gave us, smiting and deriding us withal.

They made their way steadily up the coast, mercilessly abused by Indians along the way. Miraculously, every time knives were at throats or bows were taut, some voice of restraint from another Indian or their chief kept them alive. The constant question of the Indians was *Nickaleer?*—their word for "Englishmen," whom the Indians apparently despised. Though Dickinson's party soon learned to deny it and claim they were Spanish, the Indians never believed them and would just clout them across the head until they confessed to being *Nickaleer*.

They came across the wreckage of another boat, the *Nantwich*, which had left Jamaica with them and gone aground at Fort Pierce, and met up with the survivors in the village of Jece south of Vero Beach. The chief at Jece was a wise, compassionate old man who apologized for the behavior of his southern brethren. They spent a month at this village, sticking to their story of being Spanish and the chief accepting it. Other Indians were a lot less trusting, including one who had been kidnapped by an English sloop and used as a diver on a wreck near Cuba, swam ashore at some point, escaped to Havana, was taken to St. Augustine, and made his way home. He kept inviting them to his house, and asking them the names of berries and such, to see if he could trick them into using English.

Toward the end of October they witnessed one of the great ritual dances, which made quite an impression:

> . . . all the rest are staring and scratching, pointing upwards and downwards on this and the other side every way; looking like men frighted or more like Furies: thus behaving themselves until the six have done shaking their rattles. Then they all begin a dance, violently stamping the ground for the space of an hour or more without ceasing.

They had sent one of their group northward midway through the month toward St. Augustine, and by early November a dozen Spanish soldiers came down to escort them the rest of the way. Up the Indian River, through Mosquito Lagoon, to New Smyrna Beach they traveled, on past Daytona Beach, and a horrible day near Flagler Beach where five of the group perished, unable to continue. They reached the first Spanish sentinel's house near where Marineland sits now, crossed Matanzas Inlet, and finally made St. Augustine on November 15. More than seven weeks after it began, their grueling ordeal was finally over.

Region 6

Jupiter Inlet, just south of the Palm Beach–Martin County border, is the second of the two major dividing lines along the east coast of Florida. Whereas the other one marks a difference in sand type, this inlet marks a difference in water quality. Farther north, the warm waters of the Gulf Stream run anywhere between 15 and 50 miles offshore, whereas in Palm Beach County the tropical current comes as close to the beach as 2 to 3 miles. Aside from warmer water in winter months, this also means that the water clarity is consistently much better. A constant flow of water out of the deep blue helps make these beaches some of the better ones in the state. The county has done a good job of land purchasing for public beaches, which is critical in ever-booming South Florida. If you wait too long, all the beach that hasn't been developed already becomes too expensive to purchase.

A1A's return to the beach after crossing the inlet brings you to Carlin Park, home of everything from high school cross-country races to Shakespeare by the Sea. The next few miles before the road bends inland again is a smorgasbord of beach opportunities, including Double Roads, Loggerhead Park, and Juno Beach Park, which features a brand-new fishing pier. Resuming its coastal path once again at the magnificent John D. MacArthur Beach State Park, A1A winds by Ocean Reef Park and Riviera Beach Municipal Beach before jogging inland again.

The return to the beach lands you right in the heart of Palm Beach luxury. You will be bedazzled by the conspicuous wealth and maybe tempted to drop a few thousand dollars shopping on Worth Avenue, but also perplexed at how to find a public beach. It takes a little bit of ingenuity sometimes, but it's worth it. Finally A1A stays glued to the coast, taking you through a startling variety of coastal areas. After Phipps Ocean Park and Lake Worth Pier, veritable castles are the view through the town of Manalapan, and suddenly you're back in a patch of quiet old Florida at Ocean Ridge Hammock Park. Before you know it you're passing by a community of trailer homes, of all things, at the tiny little municipality of Briny Breezes. In an election mirroring the closeness of the 2000 presidential race, seventy-seven-year-old incumbent Joe Conkey squeaked out victory over eighty-three-year-old challenger Herbert Kessman. The vote was 83 to 78. Conkey spent $11 on the race, and Kessman spent nothing. Kessman stated that he only ran against his friend because he thought contested elections were important to democracy.

Delray Public Beach gives you the first feeling of being in a town where life revolves around the beach. A half mile of public beach sits opposite a variety of shops, bars, and restaurants, yet succeeds in not being overly commercial. The coastline gets casual to the south, without much development past Atlantic Dunes Park. Condos emerge again until you get to Boca Raton, which features a few nice beaches like Red Reef Park with excellent snorkeling. Boca Raton falls somewhere in between Jupiter Island and Palm Beach in approach, having made available good beaches but charging a great deal of money for nonresidents to use them. One exception is the nice little county park on the south side of the inlet, but the only way to use the beach free in Boca Raton is to do what the locals do. Take Spanish River Boulevard from I–95 out to the beach and look for one of the free parking spaces just after you cross the bridge.

The key to enjoying the Palm Beaches is spending as much time on A1A as possible, because inland is the typical congested development of South Florida with snarled traffic or irate, speeding commuters. Out on the coast, though, life moves along at its own pleasant pace and no one's in too much of a hurry to get anywhere.

Access

I–95, the Florida Turnpike, US 1, and A1A are the main north–south arteries, though US 1 is only advisable for short distances due to congestion.

From the north, take I–95 or the Florida Turnpike to the Jupiter exit and go east to A1A.

From the south, take I–95 to Palmetto Park Road in Boca Raton and go east to A1A. Take the turnpike to exit 81 and go east on Atlantic Avenue to Delray Beach and A1A.

Beaches

Carlin Park
Juno Beach Park/Loggerhead Park
John D. MacArthur Beach State Park
Ocean Reef Park
Riviera Beach Municipal Beach
Reef Road

Phipps Ocean Park
Lake Worth Municipal Beach/Kreusler Park
Ocean Ridge Hammock Park
Delray Beach
Gulfstream Park
Red Reef Park
South Inlet Park

Other Points of Interest

Loxahatchee River—(561) 746–7053, Indiantown Road just west of I–95. Paddle this National Wild and Scenic River and see how Florida's cypress beauty has looked since time immemorial. Fish, turtles, alligators, and birds are plentiful.

Marine Life Center—(561) 966–6600. On US 1 in Loggerhead Park, Juno Beach.

South Florida Science Museum and Dreher Park Zoo—(561) 832–1988. Adjacent to I–95 just south of Southern Boulevard, West Palm Beach.

Boca Raton Inlet.

Flagler Museum—(561) 655–2833. Coconut Row and Whitehall Way, Palm Beach. Henry Flagler's opulent Palm Beach residence called Whitehall, built in 1901. Constructed of marble, the mansion has different room furnishings from all the famous European historical periods. It's not quite as extravagant as San Simeon, but it's not a hovel either.

Morikami Museum and Japanese Gardens—(561) 495–0233, off Jog Road south of Linton Boulevard, Delray Beach. Two hundred acres of bonsai trees, waterfalls, ponds, and Japanese artifacts.

Gumbo Limbo Nature Center—(561) 338–1473, across the street from the north end of Red Reef Park on west side of A1A, Boca Raton. The center is located on twenty acres of the only remaining coastal hammock in South Florida. A one-third-mile boardwalk has a 40-foot viewing tower into the canopy of the hammock. A major expansion took place in 1990 with the addition of two new educational buildings, outdoor seawater tanks for public viewing of turtles, sharks, and other sea creatures, and a Florida Atlantic University saltwater research facility. Best of all, it's free.

Gulfstream Park.

Region 6

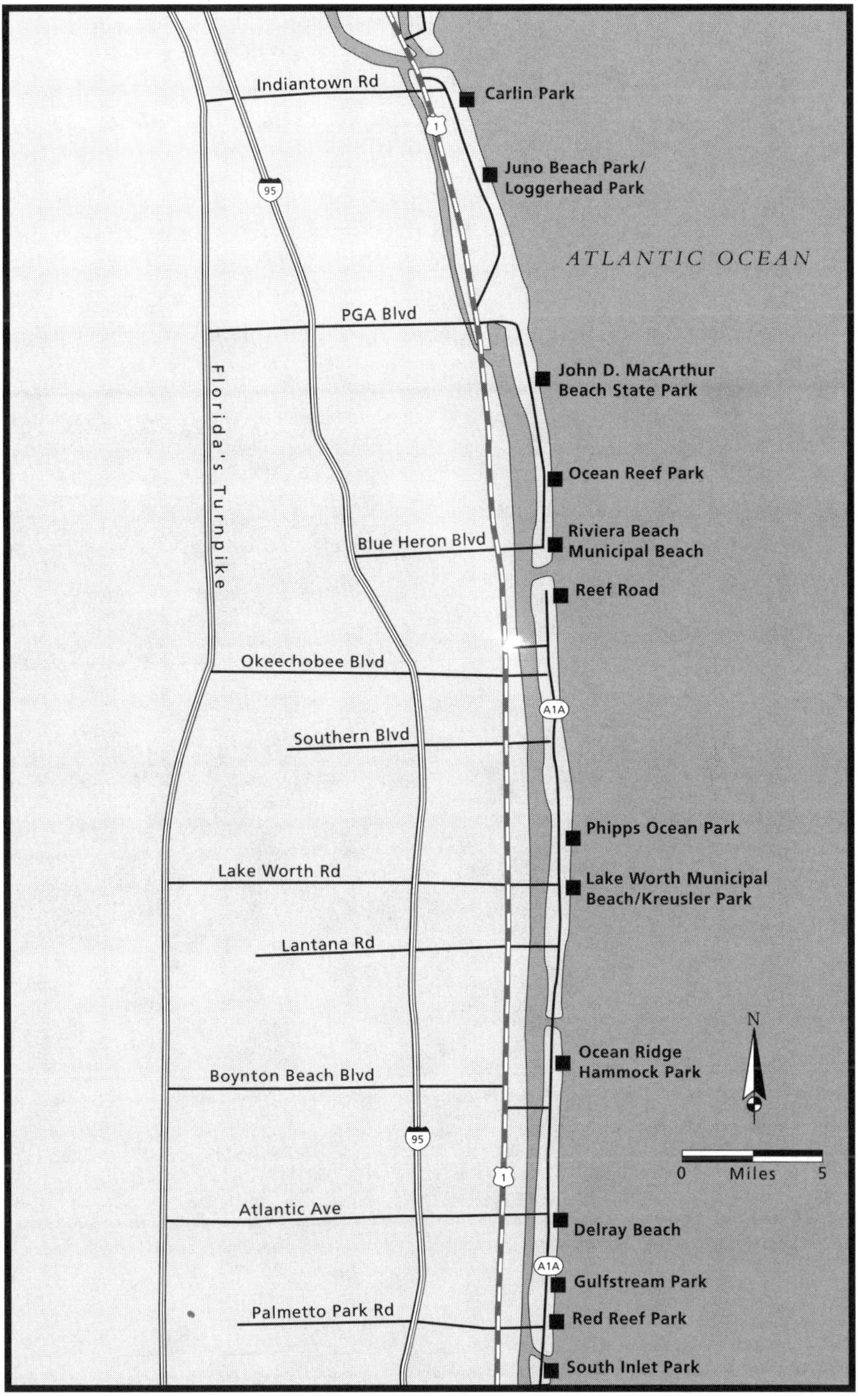

Indiantown Rd
Carlin Park
Juno Beach Park/
Loggerhead Park
ATLANTIC OCEAN
PGA Blvd
John D. MacArthur
Beach State Park
Florida's Turnpike
Ocean Reef Park
Riviera Beach
Municipal Beach
Blue Heron Blvd
Reef Road
Okeechobee Blvd
A1A
Southern Blvd
Phipps Ocean Park
Lake Worth Rd
Lake Worth Municipal
Beach/Kreusler Park
Lantana Rd
N
Ocean Ridge
Hammock Park
Boynton Beach Blvd
95
0
Miles
5
1
Atlantic Ave
Delray Beach
A1A
Gulfstream Park
Palmetto Park Rd
Red Reef Park
South Inlet Park

Carlin Park

Carlin Park is the largest beach park facility in northern Palm Beach County, encompassing 3,000 feet of guarded beach. Set back from the beach at Carlin Park are baseball diamonds, tennis courts, and soccer/football fields, along with a twenty-station exercise course. There are even bocce ball courts. Because of the enormous size of the park, it has become a favorite site for high school cross-country races over the years. Less than a half mile to the north of the beach is Jupiter Inlet, where there is yet another public park and great fishing off the south jetty, but the beach up there tends to get eroded a lot more heavily. On the north end of the beach at Carlin, elegant rock structures occasionally get exposed by the erosion of strong northeast-

Rock formations at Carlin Park.

ers. The Lazy Logger restaurant is located up toward the north end of the park, taking its name from the ubiquitous loggerhead turtles of the area.

One of the great attractions every year at Carlin Park is Shakespeare by the Sea, put on by the Palm Beach Renaissance Festival. Three long weekends in June see a Shakespeare production put on at the park, and the adaptations of the plays are usually a treat. Sometimes wildly inventive and other times traditional, the plays take advantage of the setting to great effect.

Extending south of Carlin Park is 2 miles of public beach along State Road A1A with free roadside parking. In the days when there was just dirt parking on the side of the road, this section of A1A was known as Double Roads. The beach comes and goes with storms, but always seems to be in a reasonably healthy state. It never gets crowded because of its length, though it is unguarded. Walkways descend the high dune at periodic intervals. Despite being designed to accommodate huge crowds, Carlin Park never gets all that busy—it's just so big, and there's such a glut of other good beaches to choose from around it.

ACCESS: From exit 59 off I–95 or the Jupiter exit off the Florida Turnpike, take Indiantown Road east and follow it all the way out to where it merges with A1A. Turn right onto A1A, and you will enter Carlin Park within 0.25 mile.

PARKING: There are 418 spaces at Carlin Park, and street parking along Double Roads.

HOURS/FEES: Sunrise–sunset; free.

AMENITIES: Snack bar, picnic areas, rest rooms, lifeguards, baseball diamonds, football/soccer fields, showers, fishing pier.

ACTIVITIES: Swimming, surfing, baseball, football, soccer, Shakespeare, fishing.

FOR MORE INFORMATION: Beach conditions (561) 624–0065.

Palm Beach County Parks (561) 966–6600.

Juno Beach Park/Loggerhead Park

Three miles south of Jupiter Inlet is Juno Beach Park and the Juno Beach Pier. The pier is a relatively modern facility, built in 1997, and on either side of it is 300 feet of guarded public beach. Juno had done without a pier since the early 1980s, when major storms finally vanquished the old structure. The cost to use the pier is $3.00 for fishermen, and $1.00 for others. It has also become a popular place for surfers. While surfers and pier fishermen have finally made their peace with each other in sharing the waters, another ongoing battle rages. Boats insist on violating the law that requires them to stay 500 feet away from the pier, and pier fishermen are not shy about casting sinkers at them.

Loggerhead Park is another mile south along A1A, and away from the beach it extends all the way west to front on US 1 as well. The park has a lot more off-beach facilities, including an observation tower, marine science center, and tennis courts. What is impressive about this stretch of barrier island running from Jupiter Inlet to Palm Beach Inlet is how much of it is public beach. Because the north end of Palm Beach County isn't that heavily populated, it guarantees plenty of room to lay down a towel on any given day.

ACCESS: From I–95, take exit 58 east on Donald Ross Road all the way out to the coast, turn left onto A1A, and Loggerhead Park parking will be on your left within 0.25 mile. Juno Beach Pier appears a mile farther on.

PARKING: There are 318 spaces at Juno Beach Park, 218 spaces at Loggerhead Park.

HOURS/FEES: Sunrise–sunset; free.

AMENITIES: *Juno Beach Park*—Picnic areas, rest rooms, lifeguards, showers, fishing pier. *Loggerhead Park*—Lifeguards, tennis courts, children's play area, nature trail, nature observation tower, volleyball area, marine science center.

ACTIVITIES: Swimming, surfing, fishing, tennis, volleyball, nature study.

FOR MORE INFORMATION: Beach conditions (561) 624–0065.

Palm Beach County Parks (561) 966–6600.

John D. MacArthur Beach State Park

Named after the MacArthur Dairy magnate whose foundation donated the land to the state, this is one of the finer beach state parks in South Florida. It's among the few undeveloped coastal tracts in Palm Beach County, and your last chance going south toward Miami to spend time in such a magnificent example of Florida the way it was. A boardwalk runs though an expansive mangrove estuary and sections of tropical hammock, leading out to a windswept beach with high dunes. The park encompasses more than 225 acres of land and 535 acres of water, and the 1,600-foot-long boardwalk lets you see most of it.

On the coastal side, there are good swimming and snorkeling opportunities, best in the calm summer months. There are no lifeguards on the 2 miles of beach, so use good judgment about conditions. Another attraction in summer is the nesting sea turtles, and the park has ranger-led walks on some nights. MacArthur Beach is one of the endangered green turtle's most favored nesting locations in South Florida, with 213 recorded nestings in 1998. The rare and massive leatherback, a giant among sea turtles, is an occasional visitor as well.

Back on the estuary side, there's a nature center and a nature trail, along with picnic areas, showers, and rest rooms. The fishing is excellent in the estuary, with snook and redfish being top attractions. Fishing writer Robert Baal wrote in *Florida Sportsman:*

> There have been dozens of times when, with the exception of beachgoers on the bridge, I've had the area to myself as my own private fishing domain. In fact, if someone were to blindfold you and drop you into the far reaches of the lagoon, with only the osprey and roseate spoonbills in sight, you'd be hard-pressed to believe you weren't lost in a remote Everglades backcountry site.

The tropical hammock trail that connects the different beach crossovers together is a wonder in itself. Normally people tend to cross over at the walkway by the rest rooms where the boardwalk ends, and miss out on a walk through the woods. Nestled in a narrow strip between the high dunes and the mangroves of the lagoon is a forest of mastic, sea grape, gumbo limbo, and pigeon plum. It's a beautifully cool respite from the heat of a summer beach day.

"This place is something of a well-kept secret," the tram driver said as he ferried me, the lone passenger, across the boardwalk on a glorious winter

The boardwalk at MacArthur Beach State Park.

day. The wealth of free public beach just to the north in Juno Beach takes up a lot of the crowds, but for those who prefer the quiet serenity of ancient Florida, you can't beat this park.

ACCESS: From I–95, take exit 57 east onto PGA Boulevard, and cross the US 1 intersection where PGA Boulevard becomes A1A. The park is located on A1A 2.8 miles south of this intersection.

PARKING: Large parking area.

HOURS/FEES: 8:00 A.M.–sunset; $3.25 per vehicle. William T. Kirby Nature Center is open 9:00 A.M.–5:00 P.M. daily except Tuesday.

AMENITIES: Nature center, rest rooms, showers, boardwalk, nature trails.

ACTIVITIES: Hiking, kayaking, surfing, fishing, swimming, turtle walks (summer), shell collecting, picnicking.

FOR MORE INFORMATION: John D. MacArthur Beach State Park (561) 624–6950.

Ocean Reef Park

Though a barrier island extends from Palm Beach Inlet to Jupiter Inlet, only the southern half of it is called Singer Island. This part officially begins at the MacArthur State Park, and the next great beach to the south of it is Ocean Reef Park. The park isn't far from the Colonnades Hotel, which was owned by John D. MacArthur and served as an unofficial business center for him in his old age. He commanded a regular seat in the coffee shop, spending most of his time there, and virtually anyone off the street could come to him with a proposition. Depending on MacArthur's mood, the dairy magnate would either grant the request or send the person off with a flea in his ear.

Ocean Reef Park is a pleasant county facility, popular with snorkelers because of the near-shore reef. The beach isn't as wide as the immense Riviera Beach Municipal Beach less than a mile south—which benefits from imported sand—but it's more natural. The water is warm year-round and quite clear during the calm summer months.

ACCESS: From I–95, take exit 55 east onto Blue Heron Boulevard, cross the Intracoastal Waterway, and Blue Heron turns into North A1A. A mile beyond the spot where the road curves left and heads north, Ocean Reef Park will be on your right.

PARKING: There are 240 spaces.

HOURS/FEES: Sunrise–sunset; free.

AMENITIES: Rest rooms, showers, lifeguards, picnic areas, grills.

ACTIVITIES: Swimming, snorkeling, fishing.

FOR MORE INFORMATION: Beach conditions (561) 624–0065.

Palm Beach County Parks (561) 966–6600.

Riviera Beach Municipal Beach

Sometimes when you've had a long day on the road, or you've been caught in traffic coming up from the south, you just want to get to a beach as fast as possible. You don't want to explore, you just want to get off I–95 and get out to somewhere you can relax, preferably without even having to look at a map. The main public beach on Singer Island affords you this luxury: You have only to get off the interstate and drive in a straight line until you're in the parking lot.

If you don't have a swimsuit, or you desperately need a drink, no problem. The Ocean Mall across the street from the beach has shops, bars, and restaurants. Some sandals might even be a good idea, because you don't want to make the crossing of this beach barefoot on a sizzling hot day. It's *wide*. Perhaps *voluminous* is a better word. There's so much space that there are a dozen beach volleyball courts west of the sand dunes. The swimming's good, and there are lifeguards. Much of the sand is imported—it gives the place claim to the title of widest beach in the area—but that doesn't detract from how much fun a place it is. Surfers often park here to walk down to the jetty break called Pump House at the nearby inlet, because the beach parking down at the inlet is limited to residents only.

ACCESS: From I–95, take exit 55 east onto Blue Heron Boulevard, cross the Intracoastal Waterway, and drive straight to the beach parking area.

PARKING: Metered parking lot.

HOURS/FEES: Sunrise–sunset; fifteen minutes for a quarter.

AMENITIES: Rest rooms, showers, lifeguards, volleyball courts, picnic tables.

ACTIVITIES: Swimming, volleyball, surfing, bodysurfing, people-watching.

FOR MORE INFORMATION: Riviera Beach Parks (561) 845–4070.

Reef Road

The nicest beach in the whole town of Palm Beach has one minor problem: It's miles from the nearest public parking. At the north end of this ritzy, society town, well away from the Breakers Hotel, Worth Avenue, Trump's Mar a Lago, and the other symbols of great wealth, is a beautiful stretch of sandy beach. Free from the rocks and seawalls that define much of the rest of the town's coastline, this lovely area extends from the residential street called Reef Road up to the south jetty of Palm Beach Inlet.

The prettiest clear blue water invites you to frolic, and the grainy sand crunches beneath your feet. Near the jetty the ocean is always calm, though a little farther down the beach is a popular surf break. The surfers who ride here have all their own little secrets of access; and on any day when there are waves, some unfortunate outsiders will be driving in circles, wondering where on earth you park.

Because the speed limits are slow on Ocean Boulevard, and most of it is very pleasant, the beach is an excellent one to ride a bike to while taking in the sights of Palm Beach's residential luxury. You can park at metered parking in town near the north post office around Poinciana Way, or at the municipal beach between Royal Palm Way and Worth Avenue.

ACCESS: From I–95, take exit 52 east onto Okeechobee Boulevard and cross the river, whereupon Okeechobee turns into Royal Palm Way; keep going all the way to the beach. Ride your bike or drive North A1A past the Breakers Hotel to Royal Poinciana Way, where there is more metered parking, and bike north on Ocean Drive for approximately 3 miles to Reef Road. The road veers hard left away from the coast just after you pass Reef Road, and there is a well-traipsed beach crossing right where this turn begins.

PARKING: Metered street parking.

HOURS/FEES: Twenty-four hours; fifteen minutes for a quarter, 8:00 A.M.–6:00 P.M.

AMENITIES: None.

ACTIVITIES: Biking, beachcombing, surfing, swimming, snorkeling, bodysurfing.

FOR MORE INFORMATION: Reef Road surf report http://www.swell.com.

Palm Beach Chamber of Commerce (561) 655–3282.

Phipps Ocean Park

At the southern border of the city limits of Palm Beach is the beach that time forgot. Phipps Ocean Park is the only major public beach in the entire town of Palm Beach, and it's safely shunted away from the big-money part of the town. Where some might feel that the park has been neglected, it's really the rustic state that gives the place its charm and its peacefulness.

There's a high, natural dune—somewhat rare in these parts—which affords you an elevated view of the coast. Scattered along the top of the dune are Indian chickees (pavilions thatched with palm leaves) with benches. The beach is narrow and pretty, and while it's not a good swimming spot due to the rocky shoreline, there are many tide pools to investigate.

Behind the dune is a vast, grassy area of picnic tables and grills, shaded by mighty ficus trees and palms. The fire department abuts the south end on A1A, and tucked in between it and the parking area is the first schoolhouse

Palm leaves are used to thatch small pavilions at Phipps Ocean Park.

of Palm Beach, a quaint little red building where the town settlers sent their children to be educated.

ACCESS: From I–95, take exit 50 east onto Southern Boulevard and go across the river. Turn right onto South A1A; the park will be on your left after 2 miles.

PARKING: Three hundred metered spaces.

HOURS/FEES: Twenty-four hours; fifteen minutes for a quarter.

AMENITIES: Rest rooms, showers, lifeguards, picnic areas, grills.

ACTIVITIES: Beachcombing, picnicking, swimming.

FOR MORE INFORMATION: Phipps Ocean Park (561) 585–9203.

Lake Worth Municipal Beach/Kreusler Park

To accommodate large concentrations of population—especially given ever-growing westward expansion, clear out to the edge of the Everglades in South Florida—municipalities have to take bold steps to make their chunk of coast more attractive than the rest. The city of Lake Worth has done this, and their public beach is meant to embrace outsiders. They have embellished the 1,200 feet of frontage with nearly every possible amenity the urban beachgoer could want, from a fishing pier that doubles as a popular surf break to cabanas and observation telescopes. The pier is very affordable, charging fishermen only $2.50 per day (a buck for under-twelves) and sight-seers only 50 cents.

The atmosphere here is a comforting one for northerners, as it's somewhat reminiscent of piers of the Jersey Shore and Maryland. There's an excellent restaurant on the pier, Benny's, which doesn't look like much at first glance but serves a mean breakfast. If you can remember anything of the film *Body Heat*, you might recall various beach scenes that were filmed at the Lake Worth Municipal Beach. The film was passing its location off as sort of a sleepy version of Palm Beach, for which this served well.

The beach goes on for nearly another 500 feet beyond the city boundaries, thanks to the county-run Kreusler Park next door, which has its own set of lifeguards and facilities. Between the two, there's a lot of beach here and always a lot going on. If salt water isn't for you, the Lake Worth Municipal Pool is here as well, with $2.00 admission for adults and a buck for seniors

Lake Worth Pier.

and children. Barton Park is nearby, with a playground for toddlers and children, and picnic areas shaded by sea grapes.

ACCESS: From the north, take exit 48 off I–95 to 10th Avenue North and go east to US 1. Turn right and go to Lake Avenue; turn left and cross the bridge to the beach.

From the south, take exit 47 off I–95 to 6th Avenue South and go east to US 1. Turn left, go to Lake Avenue, turn right, and cross the bridge to the beach.

PARKING: Large metered parking area, another lot at Kreusler, more on the west side of A1A.

HOURS/FEES: 6:00 A.M.–midnight; fifteen minutes for a quarter. *Kreusler*—Sunrise–sunset, twenty minutes for a quarter. *West side of A1A*—Two-dollar-a-day token parking.

AMENITIES: Fishing pier, restaurants, rest rooms, showers, lifeguards, cabanas, telescopes, municipal pool, children's playground, shuffleboard courts, picnic areas, grills.

ACTIVITIES: Swimming, surfing, fishing, shuffleboard, picnicking, dining, romance.

FOR MORE INFORMATION: Lake Worth Parks and Recreation (561) 533–7367.

Palm Beach County Parks (561) 966-6600.

Beach conditions (561) 276–3990.

Ocean Ridge Hammock Park

South of Lake Worth, beach access disappears for a while through the condos of South Palm Beach and the mansions of the tony community of Manalapan, but it resurfaces just south of Boynton Inlet. This inlet is a tiny one, which is probably why the beaches to the south of it are unaffected.

Ocean Ridge Hammock Park appears a half mile south of the inlet, with a small, nicely landscaped parking lot on the west side of A1A. There is a dirt trail through the coastal hammock out to the beach, where you pass by ficus, sea grape, gumbo limbo, and mastic. Any remains of coastal hammock right on the beach this far south are usually celebrated as a great rarity, but this is an unassuming county park kept in the old style: minimal amenities, maximum serenity. A boardwalk crosses the dune grasses out to a wide, beautiful beach that doesn't get a lot of use.

The water is the rich blue of the Palm Beaches, and always warm for swimming due to the proximity of the Gulf Stream. Just a short stroll to the north—Ocean Inlet Park—is another county park with lifeguards and facilities. Next door to the south is Boynton Public Beach, but it's essentially a residents-only beach with a $10 fee for outsiders. The stretch of beach at the hammock is the nicest part, and a good central location from which to explore in either direction.

ACCESS: Take exit 44 off I–95 east onto Boynton Beach Boulevard and go to US 1. Turn right and then left onto Ocean Avenue (SR 804), go to A1A, and turn left; the parking area will be on your left within 0.5 mile.

PARKING: Twenty-eight spaces.

HOURS/FEES: Sunrise–sunset; free.

AMENITIES: Boardwalk.

ACTIVITIES: Swimming, snorkeling, beachcombing, fishing.

FOR MORE INFORMATION: Beach conditions (561) 276–3990.

Palm Beach County Parks (561) 966–6600.

Delray Beach

This is what you call a full-service beach. At more than 7,000 feet long, the sands shimmer off for as far as the eye can see. If you're not impressed with the people-watching at one end, drive a mile down to the other end and see who rolls by. Across the street are beach shops, restaurants, hotels, bars, bank machines, and everything else you could want during a day at the beach. Rather than central locations of facilities that would involve long walks out of your way, the dozens of showers are spaced out at each beach crossing along the entire length.

The whole culture of the town of Delray Beach seems to revolve around this strip, yet it's no overblown party joint like Fort Lauderdale used to be during spring break. It just seems like a town that appreciates its beach, and

Delray Beach offers unexpected opportunities for surfing.

makes good use of it. Delray Beach is a healthy mix of all ages, and a little removed from the urban bustle of the central Palm Beaches.

Wave lovers are especially lucky here, because not only does the beach receive northern swells better than anywhere else this far south, but it also benefits from a rare phenomenon. During hurricane season, when storms are passing outside the Bahamas and the islands are blocking all the swell, the Northeast Providence Channel provides a tiny "swell window" for wave energy to pass through. These swells focus primarily on Delray Beach, where 20 miles to the north or south the ocean can be flat.

ACCESS: Take exit 42 off I–95 east onto Atlantic Avenue and go straight all the way to the coast.

PARKING: Four hundred metered spaces along the entire length.

HOURS/FEES: Twenty-four hours (except closed 11:00 P.M.–5:00 A.M. north of Atlantic Avenue); twenty minutes for a quarter.

AMENITIES: Lifeguards, rest rooms, showers.

ACTIVITIES: Swimming, surfing, bodysurfing, people-watching, in-line skating, biking.

FOR MORE INFORMATION: Delray Beach Parks (561) 243–7275.

Beach conditions (561) 272–3224.

Gulfstream Park

Wherever you go in the Palm Beaches, the county parks are always outstanding. Just south of the quiet, elderly community of Briny Breezes, Gulfstream Park is a beautiful stretch of beach with a lot to offer. A walkway climbs up the back side of steep dunes, through Australian pines and attractive native landscaping, and comes out into a well-shaded picnic area with plenty of grills and tables. The view of the beach is partially obscured by a thick wall of sea grape trees, adding to the charm. While the beach isn't that wide, the clear, warm water is the place to swim. Swimming is great and lifeguards command a clear view of all the action. At certain times of year, the lifeguards here offer surfing lessons.

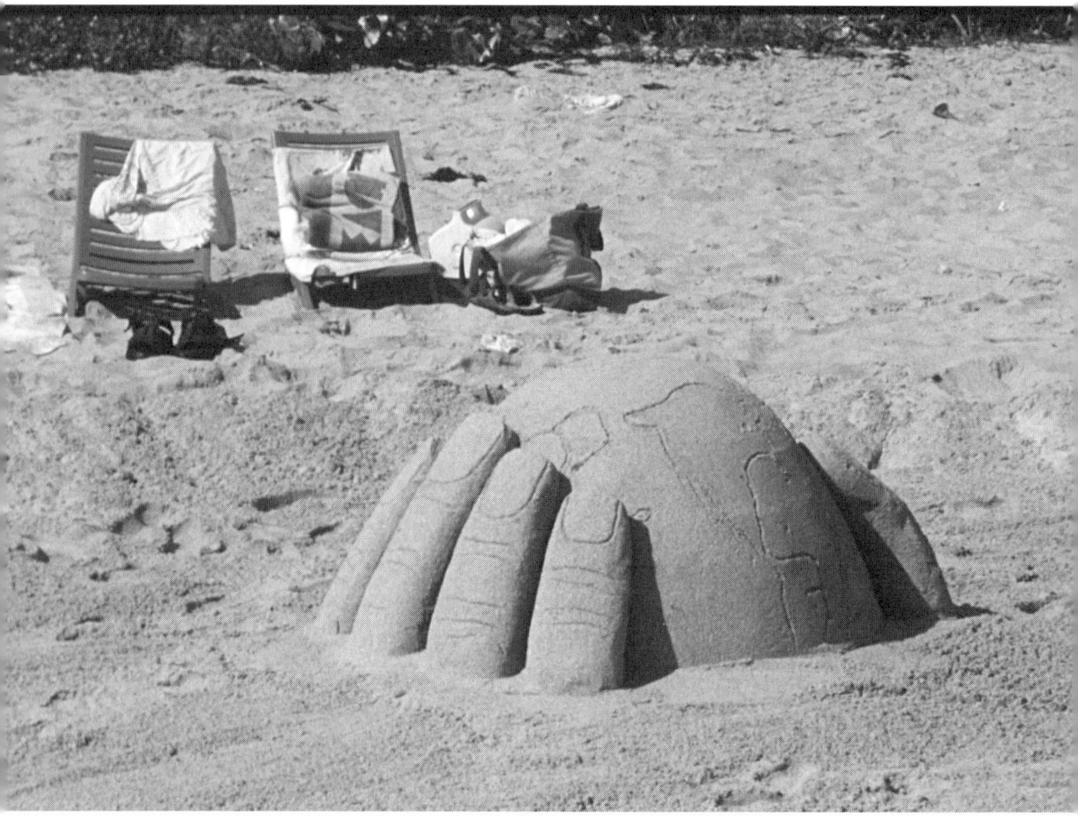

Sand sculpture at Gulfstream Park.

ACCESS: Take exit 43 off I–95 and turn east on Woolbright Road to the beach, turn right on A1A, go 1 mile—the parking area will be on your left.

PARKING: Eighty-six spaces.

HOURS/FEES: Sunrise–sunset; free.

AMENITIES: Lifeguards, rest rooms, showers, vending machines, picnic tables, grills.

ACTIVITIES: Swimming, surfing, snorkeling, sunbathing, picnicking.

FOR MORE INFORMATION: Beach conditions (561) 276–3990.

Palm Beach County Parks (561) 966–6600.

Red Reef Park

The beaches in Boca are quite good, but they're primarily meant for residents. A stiff tariff of $8.00 on weekdays and $10.00 on weekends is required for daily parking privileges. Red Reef Park is the best of these city beach parks. Sixty-seven acres of city beach park adjoin the city-owned Red Reef Executive Golf Course. The coast here is protected fairly well by the Bahamas from Atlantic storm surf, so the conditions for swimming are pretty good year-round.

An artificial reef close to shore makes it a great place to snorkel, too. The reef was built in 1988, with 600 tons of limestone sunk to create fish habitats. By all accounts, it's been a great success. There are actually seven different concentrations of artificial reef within the 5 miles of Boca's city limits, and sometimes people call the entire reef system Red Reef Park. Facilities include picnic tables and grills, a kids' play area, and a boardwalk. For those who like romantic moonlight walks in the sand, this is the only city beach open for parking after dark. The boardwalk is lighted, too.

Across the street is the Gumbo Limbo Nature Center, an excellent facility with a coastal hammock boardwalk, viewing tower, saltwater fish tanks, and classrooms. It's free, so it's definitely worth checking out.

ACCESS: Take exit 38 off I–95 east onto Palmetto Park Road all the way to the coast; turn left onto A1A and go 0.5 mile to Red Reef Park.

PARKING: Large beachside parking area.

HOURS/FEES: 8:00 A.M.–10:00 P.M.; $8.00 weekdays, $10.00 weekends, free for residents with beach permit.

AMENITIES: Rest rooms, showers, lifeguards, picnic areas, grills, children's playground.

ACTIVITIES: Swimming, picnicking, snorkeling, scuba diving, golf.

FOR MORE INFORMATION: Boca Raton Parks (561) 393–7810.

Gumbo Limbo Nature Center, 1801 North Ocean Boulevard, Boca Raton 33432 (561) 338–1473.

Greater Boca Raton Chamber of Commerce (561) 395–4433.

South Inlet Park

Boca Raton Inlet forms the northern boundary of this small and pretty beach park. An expanse of grass and walkways borders the inlet, sweeping out from A1A to the beach. While only 800 feet of beach belongs to the park, there's nothing to stop you from wandering the beach to the south. Some good snorkeling is available, and even scuba diving from the beach for the more ambitious. Fishing from the jetty will likely result in some good catches.

This beach is considerably more affordable than the city beach parks of Boca Raton, yet you still have to pay a modest fee. It is the only county beach park that charges a fee—somehow the Boca penchant for stiffing outsiders is even evident here. With limited parking, it's good to show up early on weekends. The up side is that it never gets crowded.

ACCESS: Take exit 38 off I–95 east onto Palmetto Park Road all the way to the coast; turn right onto A1A and cross the bridge over the inlet. Parking is on your left.

PARKING: Eighty-six spaces.

HOURS/FEES: Sunrise–sunset; $2.00 weekdays, $4.00 weekends.

AMENITIES: Rest rooms, showers, lifeguards, fishing jetty, nature area, children's playground, picnic shelters, grills.

ACTIVITIES: Swimming, picnicking, fishing, sunbathing, snorkeling, scuba diving.

FOR MORE INFORMATION: Boca Raton Parks (561) 393–7810.

Greater Boca Raton Chamber of Commerce (561) 395–4433.

Fishing from the jetty.

The Stream

The ocean off the Palm Beaches is defined by the Gulf Stream, through the proximity of this enormous tropical current. "The Stream"—as locals call it—begins in the Gulf of Mexico, gains definition in the Florida Straits between Key West and Cuba, and flows up the east coast. By the time it has reached the Georgia border it's well offshore, and doesn't pass close to land again until the bulge of Cape Hatteras, North Carolina. It then circulates up past Nova Scotia and across the North Atlantic, breaking up off the coasts of Ireland and Scotland.

The Stream was where Hemingway envisioned his ancient fisherman in *The Old Man and the Sea*. My father caught five swordfish, including a 370-pound behemoth, by spending many nights floating until morning in The Stream from Palm Beach to Stuart. My grandmother was towed on an undersea sled in The Stream, of which she wrote:

> Blue is all around you to infinity. There is no horizon, no bottom, only a scalloped ceiling above. You have an undersea chauffeur, plus some dolphins for company. . . . Back in the boat you are disconsolate. Air is such a sleazy product to have wrapped around your body.

The Stream brings all manner of things relentlessly north, from Cuban rafters to larval lobster that grow into the succulent "bugs" that adorn many a coastal dinner table. Suffering a breakdown in The Stream is any boater's worst nightmare, and a hundred times more so if your radio goes out. The flow of the current is so fast that by the time you get north of Fort Pierce, the search area grows large enough that it may take days of intensive searching for aircraft to locate you . . . if ever. This accounts for part of the legend of the Bermuda Triangle.

Less than a half mile off Palm Beach, reefs in 60 to 90 feet of water benefit from the closeness of The Stream. Scuba diving is as good here as anywhere else in Florida at this depth, with fantastic marine life. One of the better reefs is in 55 feet of water directly offshore from The Breakers hotel; Palm Beach even boasts one artificial reef formed by a—no, I'm not kidding—sunken Rolls-Royce. Almost as strange, there have been sailfish caught off the Juno Beach Pier.

So if you're visiting these parts, cryptically tell your friends back home that you were at an "island by The Stream," where you "dined on bugs" and went "diving for a Rolls." Leave them to figure it out.

Region 7

Coastal development grows ever heavier as you wander south into the largest urban areas of Florida, but the beaches stay lovely. Warm water year-round, plus a wealth of other opportunities beyond the beach, is why this area remains so popular.

Immediately upon entering Broward County on A1A, Deerfield Beach and the Deerfield Pier become visible. Long a favorite among area fishermen, the pier is the hub of beach life in this town. Deerfield Beach is one of a number of lazy, quiet beach communities that persist in popping up throughout South Florida. No one can accuse Broward County of being a place without pier, because just south of the Hillsboro Inlet and its historic lighthouse is another long public beach and pier in Pompano Beach.

Getting into the heart of Fort Lauderdale, Hugh Taylor Birch State Park is another typical example of the state park system preserving wild Florida in the most unlikely surroundings. Just north and south of the state park boundaries, Fort Lauderdale City Beach extends. The Strip was known in its 1980s heyday as *the* spring break destination, with hundreds of thousands of college students descending upon it each year. The original Fort Lauderdale was based in this area, a fort built in 1838 during the Seminole Wars and named after Major William Lauderdale. The fort was built in response to a Seminole Indian attack on the Colee family, who had moved up from Key West to settle here. A group of Seminole, who were irate about the Colees' displacing them from an old campsite and farming area, killed the family while the father and son were sailing to Key West. When Colee senior returned, he set out up the coast to Jupiter to obtain Major Lauderdale's soldiers to protect the region.

South of the inlet at Port Everglades is a long stretch of undeveloped beach known as the John U. Lloyd State Park. Australian pines dominate the landscape, giving it the appearance of what some call "new old Florida." Though Australian pines, or casuarinas, have been a part of the Florida beach landscape as long as most residents can remember, they are a nonnative

Deerfield Beach.

species that most state parks are attempting to rid themselves of. The atmosphere is slightly surreal as you gaze out from this oasis of undeveloped land, with the wild Atlantic to one side, the condos of Fort Lauderdale across the inlet, and the giant freighters in the port on the waterway.

Dania and Hollywood bring back a dose of the unchanged-by-time communities last seen up at Deerfield. The twenty-four-hour fishing pier at Dania Beach is a big draw, and North Beach Park is a pleasure. It keeps getting better, as the 5 miles of public beach in Hollywood is a tribute to forward thinking. The Hollywood Boardwalk, a one-lane-wide stretch of pavement for walkers, joggers, and in-line skaters, parallels the beach for the whole stretch. There is no development on the east side of A1A along here, just a succession of small parking areas. It may not be the Avenue of the Stars, but Tinseltown can only wish it had a beach like this.

Haulover Inlet County Park is the first of the great Dade County beaches, while also the last area of low-rise quietude before the condo bustle of Miami. It's an outlet for the denizens of North Miami, and has a rich history. Back in the rum-running days of Prohibition, boatloads of rum came from the Bahamas to cross the beach here. The northern part is also Florida's only official nude beach.

Access

From the north on I–95, take exit 37 east onto Hillsboro Boulevard and go all the way to the beach and A1A.

From the south on I–95, take exit 18 east onto SR 826 (Northeast 167th Street) and go all the way to the beach and A1A.

From the west on I–75, exit onto I–595 to Fort Lauderdale, then exit onto I–95 north or south and follow the directions above.

Beaches

Deerfield Beach
Pompano Beach
Hugh Taylor Birch State Park
Fort Lauderdale Beach
John U. Lloyd State Park
North Beach Park
Hollywood Beach
Haulover Beach

Camping

Hugh Taylor Birch State Park—Reservations (954) 564–4521. Group camping only. The park can take up to seventy-two people in the group camp, which has sleeper cabins, a meeting and dining room, and a fully equipped kitchen. Call for rates.

Easterlin Park—(954) 938–0610, fax (954) 938–0625, 1000 Northwest 38th Street, Oakland Park. Features include fifty-five RV and tent rental campsites, forty-five with water and electricity, as well as a shower/rest room facility, playground, and the three-quarter-mile Woodland Nature Trail. Primitive group camping is also available by reservation to nonprofit groups. There is one forty-capacity picnic shelter with grill, water, electricity, and picnic tables; additional tables and grills are located in shaded picnic areas near the park's entrance. Facilities for basketball, volleyball, and horseshoes. Thick foliage shields the park from surrounding developed areas. Cypress trees 250 years old and 100 feet tall are common in the park, which is also home to such wildlife as ducks, squirrels, and peacocks.

Quiet Waters Park—(954) 360–1315, quietwaterscamping@broward.org, 401 South Powerline Road, Deerfield Beach 33442. For new campers, as well as those without their own equipment, Quiet Waters Park offer sixteen sites with its innovative Rent-A-Camp package: a tent that sleeps up to six people, a picnic table, a grill, and running water. There are also seven other sites for campers who bring their own equipment; no RV sites are available. The park's 430 acres include one lake with a swimming beach, another for cable waterskiing, and another for boating and fishing. Other amenities include shelters, picnic areas, playgrounds, mountain bike trails, snack bar, biking/jogging path, and boat and sports equipment rentals.

Tokeepeegee Yugnee Park—(954) 985–1980, tycamping@broward.org, 3300 North Park Road, Hollywood 33021. The Whispering Pines Campground, along the eastern edge of T.Y. Park, provides sixty campsites: twelve for tents and forty-eight RV sites, each equipped with electricity, water, a grill, a picnic table, and a patio. The rest room building also includes hot showers and laundry facilities.

Other Points of Interest

Hillsboro Inlet Lighthouse—Pompano Beach. A classic old Florida lighthouse. Built in 1907, it's located between Deerfield Beach and Fort Lauderdale on the north side of Hillsboro Inlet. This 137-foot-tall octagonal, pyramidal iron skeleton tower has a metal cylinder housing the 175 stairs; the automated beacon is still active today.

International Swimming Hall of Fame—(954) 462–6536, 1 Hall of Fame Drive, Fort Lauderdale. Vintage Tarzan and Esther Williams films, Olympic competitions, and other swimming-related features at Huizenga Theatre. Gift shop, souvenirs and swimming merchandise. Noon–7:00 P.M. Monday through Friday; 9:00 A.M.–4:00 P.M. Saturday; 11:00 A.M.–4:00 P.M. Sunday. $3.00 adults; $1.00 students, citizens, and military; $5.00 family.

Ah-Tha-Ki Museum—(954) 792–0745, Seminole Indian Reservation, Stirling Road and SR 7 in Hollywood. Seminole culture and traditions. Open 9:00 A.M.–4:00 P.M. Wednesday through Sunday. Donation.

Billie Swamp Safari—Group sales (305) 257–2134; Safari Park (800) 949–6101. Take I–75 one hour west of Fort Lauderdale. Features Seminole Indian swamp buggy tours and shows in the Everglades. See gardens of palmetto, cypress, and sawgrass; spot alligators, birds, and animals. Overnight camping village and gift shop available. Open daily 9:00 A.M.–5:00 P.M.

Museum of Discovery and Science/IMAX Theater—(954) 467–6637, 401 Southwest 2nd Street, in downtown Fort Lauderdale.

Flamingo Gardens and Arboretum—(954) 473–2955, 3750 Flamingo Road, Davie/Fort Lauderdale 33330. Features a 1.5-mile guided tram tour. Includes Botanical Gardens, Everglades Wildlife Sanctuary, Wildlife Encounter, tropical plant house, aviary, Everglades museum, hummingbird garden, golden eagle exhibition. Open 10:00 A.M.–6:00 P.M. daily; $8.00, $6.40, and $4.50.

Baltimore Orioles Spring Training Center—(954) 776–1921, Fort Lauderdale Stadium, 5301 Northwest 12th Avenue, off Commercial Boulevard just west of I–95.

Pompano Beach.

Region 7

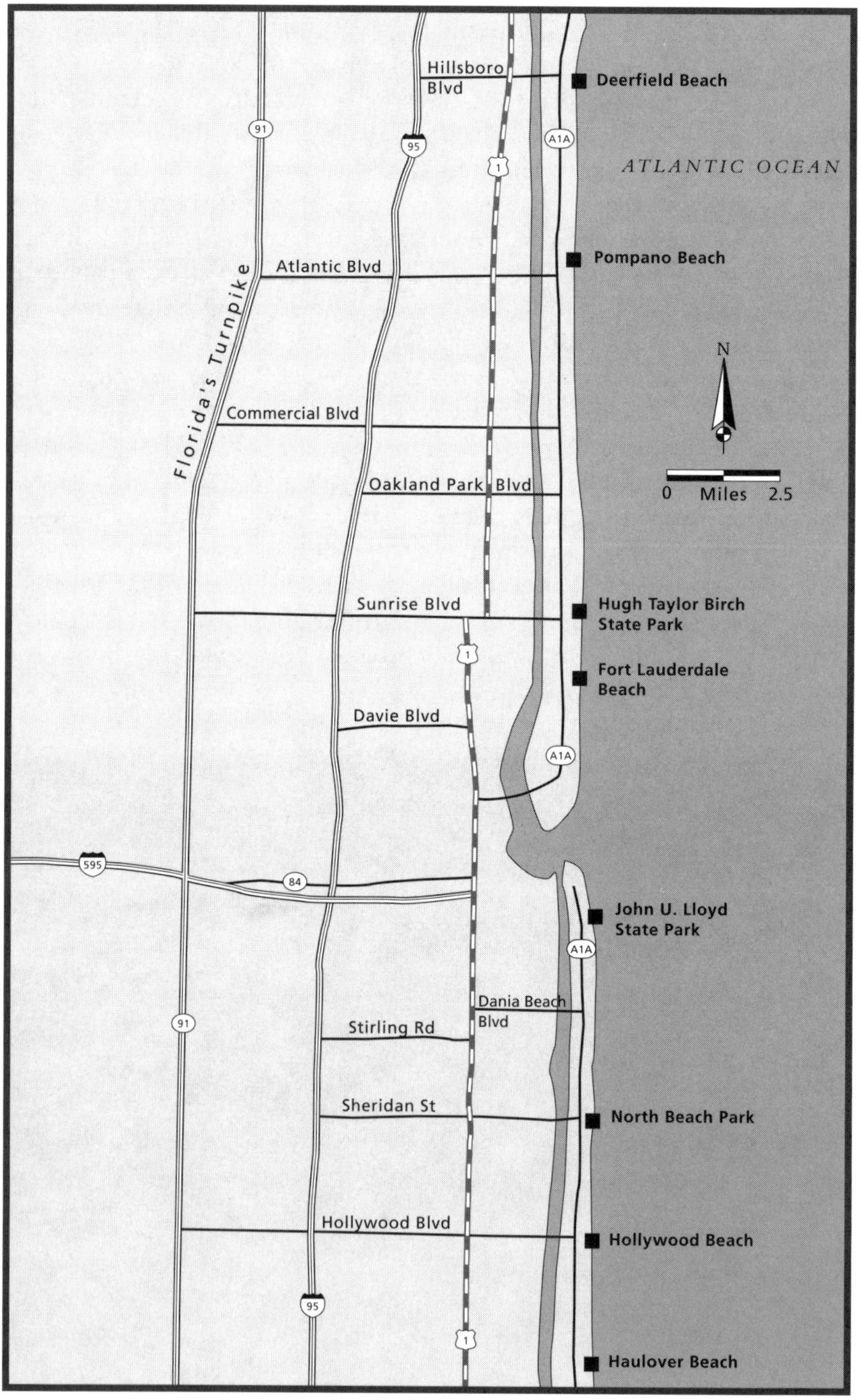
Hillsboro Blvd
Deerfield Beach
91
95
A1A
1
ATLANTIC OCEAN
Pompano Beach
Atlantic Blvd
Florida's Turnpike
N
Commercial Blvd
Oakland Park Blvd
0 Miles 2.5
Sunrise Blvd
Hugh Taylor Birch State Park
Fort Lauderdale Beach
Davie Blvd
595
84
John U. Lloyd State Park
Dania Beach Blvd
Stirling Rd
Sheridan St
North Beach Park
Hollywood Blvd
Hollywood Beach
Haulover Beach

Deerfield Beach

Deerfield Beach is a mile long, and spacious in width. A nice wooden boardwalk runs along the length of the beach; benches and covered pavilions line the grassy area beside it. The flat expanse of sand can prove a bit scorching on a hot day if you don't get to the water quickly, but cabanas and beach umbrellas are available for rental to keep your own little niche cooler. There are also palm trees and tiki huts to hide under. The Deerfield Beach Pier juts out 900 feet into the Atlantic, and is immensely popular with local fishermen. The waves near the pier are big with surfers, though often nothing but local windswells makes it here due to the shadow of the Bahamas.

Deerfield Beach has about every type of recreation you can think of, so there's plenty to keep young and old occupied with something that strikes their fancy. Kayaks and a variety of other watercraft can be rented on the south side of the pier, and there are lots of sand volleyball courts, along with a beachside walkway for skating. The surrounding atmosphere is decidedly

Hillsboro Lighthouse.

low-key, a mix of restaurants, bars, and beachwear shops. In April, professional women's beach volleyball comes to town. Other annual events include the Mango Festival in June and the Deerfield Beach Art Show in January. To the south at the Hillsboro Inlet is the Hillsboro Lighthouse, a structure built in 1907 that is the only "iron skeleton" lighthouse north of Miami on the east coast of Florida.

ACCESS: From I–95, take exit 37 east onto Hillsboro Boulevard and go all the way to the beach.

PARKING: Metered street parking.

HOURS/FEES: Sunrise–sunset; fifteen minutes for a quarter.

AMENITIES: Fishing pier, rest rooms, showers, lifeguards, cabanas, picnic areas, grills.

ACTIVITIES: Volleyball, fishing, swimming, surfing, picnicking.

FOR MORE INFORMATION: Deerfield Beach Parks and Recreation (954) 480–4412.

Beach conditions (954) 480–4413.

Pompano Beach

The beach area of Pompano Beach is something of a carbon copy of Deerfield Beach—or maybe vice versa, because the community of Pompano dates back farther in time than Deerfield. Both of them added "Beach" to the town names later on, as many coastal Florida towns have done, to make themselves more marketable. The surveyor who laid out Pompano got inspiration for the town name from dinner one night, when he "bethought himself of the toothsome fish Pompano on his plate." Between the Hillsboro Inlet and Southeast 18th Street, there's a mile of public beach, with the fishing pier located to the north of Atlantic Boulevard. The pier costs $2.50 for adults and $1.00 for children under twelve; it offers rod and reel rentals along with a bait and tackle shop.

For a half mile along the beach, a promenade gives in-line skaters a place to safely cruise, along with joggers and bicyclists. Pets are allowed on the promenade, but not on the beach. The beach is guarded from 9:00 A.M. to 5:00 P.M. every day, and the relatively abrupt drop-off to deeper water means that you need to be careful here about rip currents and undertow. On the other hand, this area is like most of Broward in that it doesn't get rough conditions often, except from local winds. Surfing at the pier is allowed only on the north side. The beach is extremely wide throughout most of its length, and beach volleyball gets pretty active on the weekends.

ACCESS: From I–95, take exit 34 east onto Atlantic Boulevard and go all the way to the beach. Turn left onto A1A (North Pompano Beach Boulevard) and go north to 222 North Pompano Beach Boulevard for the pier.

PARKING: Metered street parking, parking lots.

HOURS/FEES: Twenty-four hours; $2.00–3.00 a day in lots, 25 cents per fifteen minutes in meters.

AMENITIES: Fishing pier, bait and tackle shop, rest rooms, showers, lifeguards, picnic areas, children's playground, promenade, beach volleyball courts.

ACTIVITIES: Volleyball, fishing, swimming, surfing, picnicking, in-line skating.

FOR MORE INFORMATION: Pompano Beach Parks (954) 786–4111; www.ci.pompano-beach.fl.us.

Beach conditions (954) 786–4005.

Hugh Taylor Birch State Park

Named after pioneer Hugh Taylor Birch, this state park is one of the most urban in Florida. Right in the heart of Fort Lauderdale at the north end of the Strip, this 180-acre park is a luxurious oasis of greenery. The old homestead of Birch has become the Terramar Visitor Center, and an underpass beneath A1A leads to a 400-foot-long strip of beach patrolled by Fort Lauderdale city lifeguards. This means no surfing during lifeguard hours, but there are plenty of other beaches where you can do that.

In the main section of the park, between A1A and the river, a small lagoon meanders through the mangroves. Canoe rentals are available here, and it's easy to forget as you paddle along that you're only a short distance from where the most depraved mob havoc in the world used to take place during spring break. A 1.7-mile exercise course for hikers and runners wraps around the edge of the park. For large groups desiring an outdoor conference setting with ready access to the big city, a group camp is available with cabins, a meeting room, and kitchen.

ACCESS: From I–95, take exit 30 east onto Sunrise Boulevard and go all the way to the beach. The entrance will be on your left.

PARKING: Ample parking within the park, free street parking on A1A outside the park.

HOURS/FEES: 9:00 A.M.–5:00 P.M. on the beach, 8:00 A.M.–sunset in the rest of the park; $3.25 per vehicle, $1.00 walk-in or ride-in.

AMENITIES: Rest rooms, showers, lifeguards, picnic areas, grills.

ACTIVITIES: Sunbathing, biking, canoeing, fishing, swimming, in-line skating.

FOR MORE INFORMATION: Hugh Taylor Birch State Park (954) 564–4521.

Fort Lauderdale Beach

Though they don't host the annual madness that they used to back when Fort Lauderdale was synonymous with spring break, the Fort Lauderdale city beaches are more popular than ever on a year-round basis. As far back as 1953, 15,000 students a year were coming for spring break, and the event really achieved notoriety after 1960 when the George Hamilton film *Where the Boys Are* was released. At the height of its popularity in 1985, 350,000 students were crushing into town for the annual bacchanalia. That was the year the town decided it had had enough, and actively discouraged spring breakers from visiting in the future. The move appeared to be a wise one, because the area has flourished without the influx. Unlike the small-town resorts with large hotel capacity that host the bulk of spring breakers these days—Daytona Beach, South Padre Island, and Panama City—Fort Lauderdale is now a thriving metropolis that doesn't need the extra business. Despite some grumblings that the area was going upscale, it's still a youth-friendly city, and if anything has a more diverse nightlife scene than its much larger neighbor to the south, Miami.

Three different sections of beach run for 4 miles from Oakland Park Boulevard down to the jetty at Port Everglades. All of them boast plentiful amounts of sand from beach renourishment efforts, with the most at the

Fort Lauderdale Beach.

southern end. The infamous Strip runs from Sunrise Boulevard down to Las Olas Boulevard, and is far and away the busiest section. The northern section of municipal beaches runs from Oakland Park Boulevard to Northeast 20th Street. It's quieter but doesn't have as many facilities; the same holds true for the section down by the jetty at the south end. One of the nice things about the most of the Lauderdale beaches—and it's always refreshing to find in an urban setting—is that there's no development on the beach side of A1A. As soon as you've found your parking spot, you have an unobstructed view of the beach and surf and can choose accordingly where you want to go.

What immediately catches your attention along the central stretch is the winding wall that borders the wide sidewalk, where people skate, jog, and bicycle along. The wall runs for a few miles from Sunrise Boulevard south to the Yankee Clipper Hotel. Within the wall is a fiber-optic cable; at night it projects a light that changes color every six seconds. Volleyball and basketball courts can be found here, along with a fitness course.

ACCESS: From I–95, take exit 30 onto Sunrise Boulevard and go all the way to the beach. The main beach begins south of Sunrise. To access the northern beaches, either drive a short distance north on A1A or take the Oakland Park Boulevard exit (exit 31) from I–95 all the way to the beach.

PARKING: Street parking on A1A, municipal parking area at Las Olas and Ocean Boulevards.

HOURS/FEES: Twenty-four hours; free angled parking on A1A, metered street parking, $6.00 per day in the municipal lot.

AMENITIES: Volleyball courts, basketball courts, rest rooms, showers, lifeguards, picnic tables, concessions, fitness course.

ACTIVITIES: Volleyball, basketball, sunbathing, biking, swimming, in-line skating, jogging.

FOR MORE INFORMATION: Fort Lauderdale Beach (954) 468–1595.

John U. Lloyd State Park

In a completely different world than urban Fort Lauderdale is the sprawling state park on the south side of Port Everglades. Rangy Australian pines billow in the breeze, and a long, narrow ribbon of secluded beach greets you. The beach is almost 2.5 miles long, and a great one for those who like strolling the water's edge for long distances. It can suffer from typical south-of-inlet erosion, so there's not that much room to spread out at the northern end, but farther south the beach is ample. The jetty is used by fishermen; the rest of the park is used by not a whole lot of anyone. A nature trail winds through the Australian pines and sea grapes, and canoes and kayaks are available for rental to explore around the mangroves of the Intracoastal. A boat ramp is situated at the north end, allowing easy access to the ocean through the inlet at Port Everglades. Coco's Café is the park's main food concession, a pleasant place offering standard fare.

During the 1960s this was one of the locations used by military divers of the Underwater Demolition Team for training, and there are some remains of the underwater obstacle courses offshore. Sandwiched up against the inlet are a few remaining navy buildings where research is done. The entire area parcel was owned by the military until the state bought it, which accounts for the relaxed look of benign neglect that it shares with another former UDT training area, Fort Pierce Inlet State Recreation Area.

ACCESS: From I–95, take exit 24 east on Stirling Road to US 1. Turn left and go two blocks to Dania Beach Boulevard (South A1A); turn right and go all the way to the beach. The park entrance will be on your left after you cross the Intracoastal Waterway.

PARKING: Multiple parking lots.

HOURS/FEES: 8:00 A.M.–sundown; $1.00 per hiker or biker, $2.00 per single-occupant vehicle, $4.00 per vehicle with two to eight passengers.

AMENITIES: Rest rooms, showers, food concession, picnic tables, grills, nature trail.

ACTIVITIES: Canoeing, hiking, biking, swimming, fishing, boating, snorkeling, in-line skating, jogging.

FOR MORE INFORMATION: John U. Lloyd State Park (954) 923–2833.

North Beach Park

At this Broward County park just to the north of the Hollywood city beaches, sand dunes and tall strands of seagrass are nurtured to ensure their preservation. Actually, sand dunes are an extreme rarity in this part of Florida—most were bulldozed away long ago—so it's a nice attempt to recapture the natural condition of this coast. The fifty-six acres feature a paved bike path, along with an observation tower and playground. On the Intracoastal Waterway there's a boardwalk, and river fishing can be done there. Sports equipment is available for rent, and you'll also find a snack bar.

ACCESS: From I–95, take exit 23 east onto Sheridan Road all the way to the beach.

PARKING: Large lot.

HOURS/FEES: 8:00 A.M.–sunset; $5.00 per vehicle weekends, $3.00 weekdays.

AMENITIES: Rest rooms, showers, lifeguards, picnic tables, bike path, snack bar, riverside boardwalk.

ACTIVITIES: Sunbathing, biking, volleyball, swimming, jogging, river fishing.

FOR MORE INFORMATION: North Beach Park (954) 926–2444.

Hollywood Beach

Hollywood was originally conceived with the same ambition as Jacksonville, but on a smaller scale. In any event, the plans fell short of the mark. Where Jacksonville was originally designed to be Florida's Los Angeles, with city limits all the way to the county line to accommodate the boom that never happened, Hollywood was built by a speculator from California who envisioned an exclusive enclave for the rich like Palm Beach. There was nothing wrong with the setting: gorgeous beaches, a quiet community, Miami far enough away yet still close by... but Florida has been the doom of many who've tried too hard to mold it to their visions. In the second half of the twentieth century, South Florida beach communities simply fell out of favor. Miami Beach wilted and faded, Fort Lauderdale stayed sort of pokey, and retirees and snowbirds looked elsewhere.

While Lauderdale and Miami Beach eventually changed their fortunes, Hollywood has remained charmingly stuck in time. It by no means seems neglected, but has a fresh look of 1960 to it rather than a fresh new millennium look. The main public beach is a 2.5-mile stretch, with a 27-foot-wide promenade for walkers, joggers, in-line skaters, and bicyclists called the Hollywood Broadwalk, though the entire length of beaches in Hollywood extends some 5 miles.

You can rent bicycles and in-line skates right on the Broadwalk. There is no development on the beach side of A1A, just lots of street-end parking and the wide Broadwalk for cruising. On the beach, planted palm trees provide nooks of shade while looking just a little like props on a movie set. You almost expect to see Gidget yelling "Surf's up!" and charging toward a waveless ocean, before switching to the next close-up take where she stands on the beach waving her arms while being sprayed with a hose.

"Surfs Up!" at Hollywood Beach.

ACCESS: From I–95, take exit 22 east onto Hollywood Boulevard and go all the way to the beach.

PARKING: Street-end metered parking.

HOURS/FEES: Twenty-four hours; $1.00 per hour.

AMENITIES: Rest rooms, showers, lifeguards, picnic tables, boardwalk.

ACTIVITIES: Sunbathing, biking, swimming, in-line skating, jogging.

FOR MORE INFORMATION: Beach conditions (954) 921–3334.

Haulover Beach

The north side of Haulover Inlet features an enormous county park and marina, with enough parking to handle the largest holiday crowds. Lifeguard stands are spaced out along the beach, and the area by the jetty is especially nice. The jetty hooks around at the tip, creating a small area sheltered from wave action. Both sides of the inlet are popular with surfers, because it's one of the few beaches in Miami with enough of a deep-water approach to provide strong surf, though it's not that common. Fishermen also make good use of the jetties. Located on the lagoon side, the full-service marina offers charter boat fishing and kayak rentals.

At the north end of the park is a real rarity: 800 yards of the 1.3-mile beach have been set aside and marked with signs as a nude beach. This is the only nude beach in Florida demarcated by government signs, and one of only a handful in the entire country. Almost all of America's nude beaches are a sort of wink-and-nod arrangement as far as legality goes, but this one is official. Because so many Europeans visit South Florida in winter—people accustomed to clothing being optional at beaches—Miami–Dade County saw that such a place was necessary and good for tourism. Gawkers even get escorted off the beach by patrollers. It is somewhat ironic that the nude beach at Haulover is located at the edge of Broward County, where thong-bikini wearers and topless bathers have had constant run-ins with the law.

ACCESS: From I–95, take exit 18 east onto SR 826 (Northeast 167th Street) and go all the way to the beach, passing by Oleta River State Park and crossing Sunny Isles Causeway. Turn right onto A1A and go south 0.8 mile to the north/nude beach entrance or 1.8 miles to the main entrance.

PARKING: Huge lot at the main entrance, smaller lot at the north beach.

HOURS/FEES: Sunrise–sunset; $4.00 per vehicle.

AMENITIES: Rest rooms, showers, lifeguards, picnic tables, boardwalk.

ACTIVITIES: Nude sunbathing, surfing, volleyball, kayaking, swimming, fishing.

FOR MORE INFORMATION: Haulover Beach (305) 944–3040.

Dive Sites (305) 375–DERM; http://www.metro-dade.com/derm/artificial_reef_list.html; http://www.south-florida.com/sites.html.

Haulover Marina (305) 945–3934.

Urban Trails Kayak (305) 947–1302.

Wreck Diving

The area around Haulover Beach has a rich history, dating all the way back to 1823 when a fellow named Baker used to ply the reefs for sponges. The beach became known as Baker's Haulover, because he hauled his boat over the beach and into the river. Other spongers and fishermen came to do the same; eventually a century of this practice went by before Baker's Haulover Inlet was dug in 1925 to allow easy access to the ocean. *Easy* is a bit of a relative term, though, because it's a short, narrow gap hitting deep water quickly, and the inlet can be ferocious during stormy conditions. More than one big charter boat has ended up on the rocks there. The opening of the new inlet improved the health of the north end of Biscayne Bay, and—more importantly for those seeking ways around Prohibition—allowed rum-runners coming across from the Bahamas another inlet to smuggle their illegal bounty through. Over time the "Baker's" possessive has been dropped from the name; most people just call it Haulover. It's easy to recognize those who've been around Florida for a while by whether they call the beach or the inlet "Baker's Haulover."

Diving has remained popular on the area reefs, and wreck diving has added to the number of dive sites available. Freighters, barges, oil rig towers, and other sundry vessels have been dispatched to the sea bottom off Fort Lauderdale, Haulover, and Miami Beach to create artificial reefs. Captain Rick Smith of Undersea Miami has created a dive called Wreck Trek, which links together an artificial reef area consisting of a number of wrecks. At a reasonable depth for intermediate divers—between 45 and 60 feet—the area contains a pair of tugboats, old radio towers, a steel barge, limestone boulders, and more sites being connected. A group of forty-ton army tanks from the Vietnam years is part of the trek now, as well as the freighter *Matthew Lawrence*.

What would be derelict eyesores on land have been converted by nature into something fascinating. It's a spooky feeling gliding along among some of these wrecks, though—diving, say, into the innards of a freighter. Surprises are always just around the corner, whether they be a large green moray, a sleeping nurse shark, or a huge jewfish. Your bubbles ricochet off the hull above you before finding their way to the surface. A regression seems to occur to your childhood, where everything is interesting and needs to be explored. By the time you're done, you want to develop gills so you're not limited by silly things like scuba tanks.

Region 8

Through the exclusive shops of Bal Harbor, well known as the favorite shopping district of the hoi polloi, and the condos of Surfside, public beaches are hard to find on A1A. But then, just when you might begin to despair, a mirage appears before you. Can it be? Eight blocks of undeveloped beach, shady sea grape trees, luxurious greenery, fitness trails, and more? North Shore Open Space Park is definitely one of the hidden jewels of the Miami beach scene. A dozen blocks south is 65th Street Park, a very small and pretty public beach.

The next stop marks the night-and-day difference between the quiet old Jewish neighborhoods of North Miami Beach and the new Miami. *South Beach*—two seemingly generic words strung together—immediately defines a location and scene to people all across the world. Redeveloped by entrepreneurs who saw the potential of restoring colorful art deco hotels into world-class fashion joints, South Beach transformed within five years from a forgotten, dilapidated area to one of the world's number one hot spots. When the young go out to party in Miami, it's either to Coconut Grove or South Beach. Bikini models strut the beaches surrounded by photo crews, glitterati like Madonna own dance clubs that try to re-create Studio 54's selectivity, gay men flex their oiled muscles . . . South Beach is not the place for the shy and retiring type.

Though you take your life into your hands by jockeying for position on I–95 in Miami, the drive through downtown to the Rickenbacker Causeway pays off when you leave the madness behind and reach Virginia Key and Key Biscayne. Aside from popular attractions like the Miami Seaquarium—the original home of Flipper—the two keys contain some of Miami's most gorgeous and spacious beaches with Virginia Key, Crandon Park, and Bill Baggs State Park.

Routing back to the mainland again, the hectic traffic of US 1 is best avoided in favor of Old Cutler Road along Biscayne Bay. You wind through the festive community of Coconut Grove and a lot of beautiful and expen-

Art deco guard tower at South Beach.

sive old homes before getting down to the lush greenery of Matheson Hammock County Park. Here you can shake off the sand, shower, put on some fresh clothing, and enjoy fine dining only 100 feet away. The rest of mainland Florida heading south toward the Florida Keys consists of the mangrove shallows of Biscayne Bay, with beaches in Biscayne National Park accessible only by boat. Ragged Keys, Sands Key, and Elliott Key are beautiful places to snorkel and kayak, and camping is available.

Access

From the north—Exit I–95 east on SR 922 (Northeast 125th Street) and go all the way to the beach. Turn right (south) onto A1A.

From the south—Take US 1 up from the Florida Keys into Miami.

From the west—Coming from Naples, take the Tamiami Trail to the Palmetto Expressway (SR 826), go north, and take SR 836 east to I–95.

Beaches

North Shore Open Space Park
65th Street Beach
South Beach
Virginia Key Beach
Crandon Park Beach
Cape Florida/Bill Baggs State Park
Matheson Hammock Beach Park
Biscayne National Park

Camping

Boca Chita Key Campground, Biscayne National Park—(305) 230–7275, by boat from Homestead Bayfront Park. Open, waterside, grassy camping area with picnic tables and grills. Toilets are available on the island, but there are no sinks, showers, or drinking water. To arrange for transportation to the island with the park's concessioner, call (305) 230–1100. Fees: $10 per night per site; $15 if you have a boat in the harbor.

Elliott Key Campground, Biscayne National Park—(305) 230–7275, by boat from Homestead Bayfront Park. Waterside and forested camping areas on a 7-mile-long island. Picnic tables and grills are available. Rest rooms with sinks and cold-water showers are available. Drinking water is available on the island, but bring some of your own as a precaution should the system go down. To arrange for transportation to the island with the park's concessioner, call (305) 230–1100. Fees: $10 per night per site; $15 if you have a boat in the harbor.

Other Points of Interest

Joe's Stone Crab—(305) 673–0365, 227 Biscayne Street, on the southern tip of South Beach. Joe's is a legendary institution—dating back to 1913—specializing in a unique South Florida seafood delicacy. It's open only during stone crab season (October 16 through May 14).

Oleta River State Park—(305) 919–1846, 3400 Northeast 163rd Street, North Miami. This large state park on the mainland side of the Intracoastal Waterway is primarily mangrove habitat, with riverside beaches and off-road trails for mountain bikes.

Miami Seaquarium—(305) 361–5705, 4400 Rickenbacker Causeway, Key Biscayne. Thirty-eight acres of marine-life entertainment and education. The Seaquarium is home to Lolita the killer whale, Salty the sea lion, and famous TV superstar Flipper.

Metrozoo—(305) 251–0400, 12400 Southwest 152nd Street, Miami. Having nearly 300 developed acres on a 740-acre parcel of land, this is the only zoo in the continental United States located in a subtropical climate. It houses more than 700 wild animals in a cageless environment.

Monkey Jungle—(305) 235–1611, 14805 Southwest 216th Street, Miami. Visitors stroll through enclosed paths, while the monkeys roam freely within large enclosures.

Museum of Science and Space Transit Planetarium—(305) 854–4247, at 3280 South Miami Avenue, Miami. The museum has more than 150 hands-on exhibits, plus a natural history gallery. The planetarium changes exhibits, and features a laser and star show daily. The observatory opens Saturday 8:00 A.M.–10:00 P.M. (weather permitting), offering free telescopic viewing.

Parrot Jungle and Gardens—(305) 666–7834, Southwest 57th Avenue and Southwest 112th Street, Miami. Features parrots, exotic birds, flamingos, and more in a subtropical jungle.

Vizcaya Museum and Gardens—(305) 250–9133, 3251 South Miami Avenue, Miami. This Italian Renaissance–style villa built in 1916 has thirty-four rooms of antique furnishings and decorations from the fifteenth through nineteenth centuries. The grounds include ten acres of formal gardens and fountains divided by hedges and walls.

Fairchild Tropical Garden—(305) 667–1651, 10901 Old Cutler Road, Miami. This botanical garden established in 1938 is an eighty-three-acre tropical paradise offering an extensive collection of rare tropical plants.

Bass Museum—(305) 673–7530, 2121 Park Avenue, Miami Beach. Located in a relaxed park setting in the heart of South Beach, the museum offers contemporary and historic art from throughout the world. Includes religious paintings and sculptures from the Middle Ages.

Fruit and Spice Park—(305) 247–5727, 24801 Southwest 187th Avenue, Homestead. This park offers more than 500 varieties of exotic and subtropical fruit, nut, spice, and herb trees and shrubs. Daily guided tours and naturalist workshops, plus a gourmet and fruit gift store.

The Gold Coast Railroad Museum—(305) 253–0063, 12450 Southwest 152nd Street, Miami. Features the *Ferdinand Magellan*, a luxurious railway car built for Franklin Delano Roosevelt, now a National Historic Landmark. Historic railroad cars are on display on a half mile of real track, also authentic engines, Pullmans, and dining cars.

Region 8

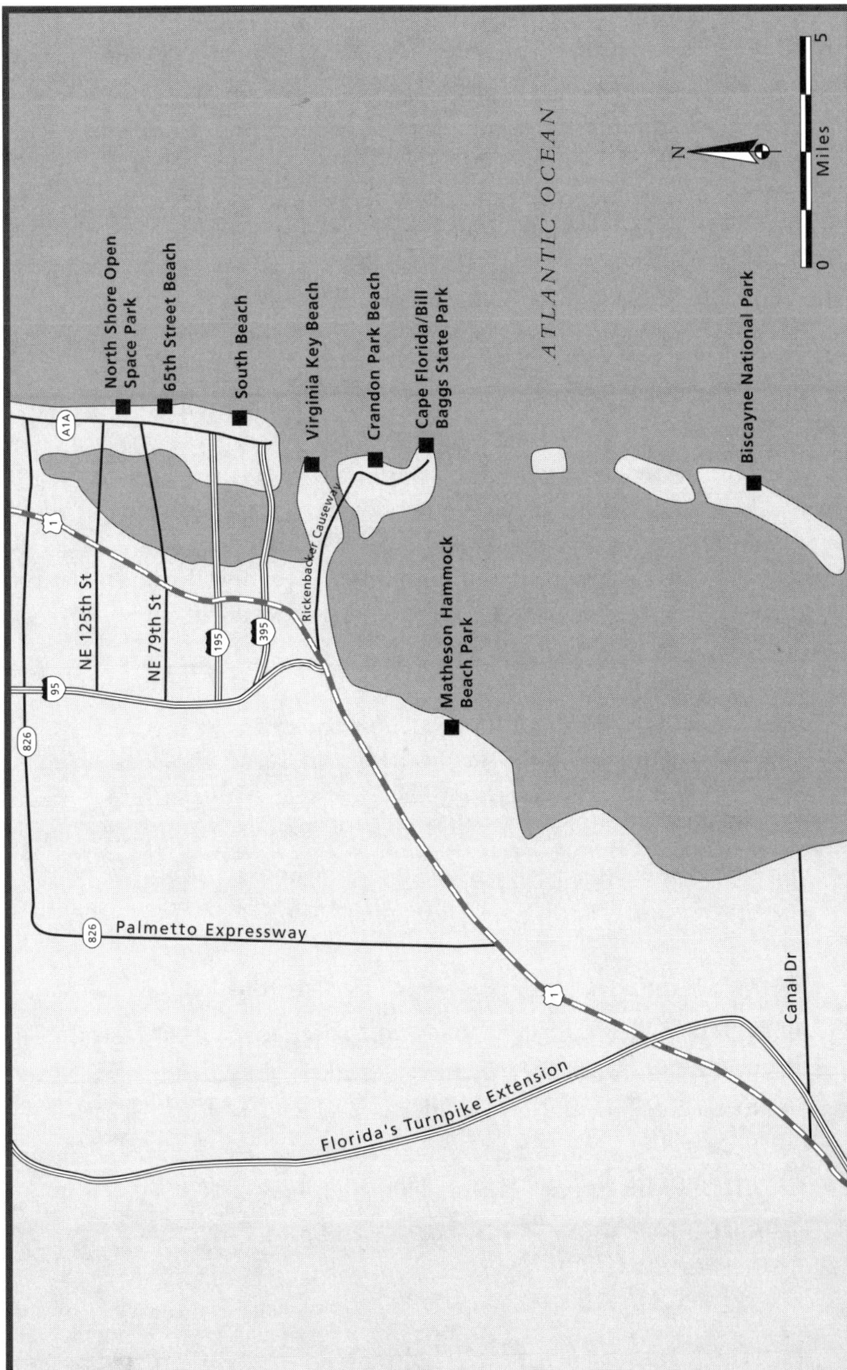
North Shore Open Space Park
65th Street Beach
South Beach
Virginia Key Beach
Crandon Park Beach
Cape Florida/Bill Baggs State Park
ATLANTIC OCEAN
N
0
5
Miles
Biscayne National Park
Matheson Hammock Beach Park
Rickenbacker Causeway
NE 125th St
NE 79th St
A1A
1
195
395
95
826
Palmetto Expressway
Canal Dr
Florida's Turnpike Extension

North Shore Open Space Park

This beach and park is one of the most unexpected surprises of North Miami Beach. Covering eight blocks and some forty acres, it is an abrupt shock of greenbelt amid the towering condos. Large ficus and sea grape trees provide plenty of shade throughout the grassy park, and there are picnic tables scattered about under these natural canopies. Plenty of sandy beach is available and the water tends to remain shallow well offshore, so it is a great place to swim. For the handicapped, the main lifeguard tower has "surfchairs" that roll through the sand, enabling wheelchair users to get around easily. Lifeguards are on duty from 9:00 A.M. to 5:00 P.M.

The food concession opens at 11:00 A.M., and aside from the usual fare you can buy beer and cigarettes. For those with fitness in mind, a series of stations with exercise instructions guide you through a full-body workout. The park can be pretty busy on weekends, but on weekdays remains a quiet place off the beaten path. Part of the reason for its excellent layout is that it used to be a state recreation area, and state parks are uniformly outstanding at preserving original old Florida conditions. The state decided to let the city lease it, and thus the entrance fee is only a buck. For a while the city let the maintenance go by, but lately they've added a series of additional rest room/changing rooms and spruced up the park.

ACCESS: From the north on I–95, exit east onto SR 922 (Northeast 125th Street) and go all the way to the beach. Turn right (south) onto A1A and go 1.5 miles to anywhere between 87th and 79th Streets.

From the south on I–95, exit east at Northwest 79th Street, cross the North Bay Causeway, turn left (north) onto A1A, and go a dozen blocks to the park.

PARKING: Metered street parking, some free street parking.

HOURS/FEES: 7:00 A.M.–8:00 P.M.; metered parking $1.00 per hour; $1.00 entrance fee per person.

AMENITIES: Rest rooms, showers, lifeguards, picnic tables, bike path, fitness course.

ACTIVITIES: Picnicking, swimming, biking, walking, exercising.

FOR MORE INFORMATION: North Shore Open Space Park (305) 993–2032.

65th Street Beach

A dozen blocks south of North Shore is a small public beach called 65th Street Park. The beach is actually about 100 yards south of 65th Street, and covers one and a half acres. It's the only obvious public beach access between South Beach and North Shore, where you can see the beach and water from A1A. It has lifeguards and basic facilities, and is a good beach to go to if you're looking for one of the quieter spots on Miami Beach. While there is a metered parking lot, there's often plenty of free street parking along A1A. The beach is expansive, the sand is beautiful, and the ocean is shallow and great for swimming.

ACCESS: From I–95, exit east onto Northwest 79th Street, cross the North Bay Causeway, turn right (south) onto A1A, and almost immediately you will be at 65th Street.

From South Beach, follow A1A north 3 miles to 65th Street.

PARKING: Metered street parking, some free street parking

HOURS/FEES: 5:00 A.M.–midnight; metered parking $1.00 per hour.

AMENITIES: Rest rooms, showers, lifeguards.

ACTIVITIES: Sunbathing, swimming.

FOR MORE INFORMATION: Miami Beach Parks and Recreation (305) 673–7730.

South Beach

If you've been seduced by the glamorous image of Miami Beach's South Beach that has kept it a *destination* in magazines throughout the world, your first impression of the real thing might leave you disappointed. The conversion process of turning a decaying community into a vibrant international hot spot has been remarkable, certainly, but it's a process that's still under way. The area between 7th and 14th Streets has undergone a nearly complete makeover, and it continues to spread to the north and south. At its most striking is the beachside street Ocean Drive, between 8th and 12th Streets, where art deco hotels like the Colony and the Ocean Front stand elegantly, and the finest restaurants do business.

During the day, the beach is the location for countless model photo shoots and more perfectly honed bodies than you can imagine. At one section up around 12th or 13th Street, it looks as if you've walked into a male model convention: hundreds of rippling muscles lie side by side, in bodies most men can only dream of. Back on the promenade, passing bicyclists say things to each other such as, "Doesn't it concern you carrying around $5,000?" and "No, I have to have ready cash."

The beach is enormous, dotted periodically with lifeguard towers painted in the same deco colors as the hotels. Volleyball courts are plentiful around 10th Street, adjacent to the promenade. The latter is a fine place to in-line or longboard skate, if you want to check people out and be checked out. The cast of diverse characters that make up South Beach always keep it entertaining; it has been an invaluable addition to the troubled identity of greater Miami.

ACCESS: From I–95, exit east at I–395; be careful to stay in the lane with the signs for Miami Beach, because the spaghetti over- and underpasses get confusing here. Cross the MacArthur Causeway, turn left (north) onto Collins Avenue (A1A), and go to anywhere between 5th and 15th Streets.

PARKING: Metered street parking; municipal garages on 7th through 13th Streets between Collins and Washington Avenues.

HOURS/FEES: 5:00 A.M.–midnight; metered parking and garages $1.00 per hour.

AMENITIES: Rest rooms, showers, lifeguards, promenade, volleyball courts, rental chairs and umbrellas.

ACTIVITIES: Topless sunbathing, in-line skating, swimming, volleyball, being fabulous.

FOR MORE INFORMATION: Miami Beach Parks and Recreation (305) 673–7730.

Virginia Key Beach

Most people crossing the Rickenbacker Causeway are headed either to the Miami Seaquarium, to Key Biscayne for the vast expanse of Crandon Park, or to the state park at Cape Florida. A forgotten beach is the lovely oceanside beach at Virginia Key, which due to the city of Miami's financial troubles in the past decade was open on an off-and-on basis. It's the city's only beach, actually, which accounts for the differing fees for residents and nonresidents. After you turn off Crandon Boulevard opposite the Seaquarium and come upon the entrance gate, it's not a bad idea to ask for directions to the beach. Otherwise you might dead-end at the wastewater treatment plant on another part of the key, thinking this author has played a cruel joke on you.

There are eight parking areas along the road out to the beach, plus a final one beachside. If you get there early, especially on a weekday, you should be able to grab one of the beachside spaces. Sailboarders flock to both here and Crandon Park, and *Windsurfer* magazine said that Virginia Key is "considered one of the top 10 places in the country to windsurf. The beach is located on the Atlantic Ocean and is protected by a sandbar just offshore. The inside of the sandbar is a great place for bump-and-jump and slalom sailing, and the sandbar offers nice wave sailing." Fishing is prohibited but it's a fine swimming beach, with shallow, sheltered waters.

One of the more intriguing fixtures of Virginia Key is Jimbo's, a ramshackle sort of building just beyond the public beach on the right. The story behind it is that a movie was filmed on the key, and the sets were left in place. Over time Jimbo turned the lumber into a makeshift bar where you can get cold ones for a buck and occasionally some fish. It looks like a place that should be condemned, but like many things on Virginia Key, the hand of authority has not had the resources to pay attention to it. Having become such a popular local fixture, Jimbo has sort of grandfathered himself into quasi-legality. It's a nod to the wild and colorful ocean history that the pioneers of Miami lived, leaving him be out there. Some of his critics feel he's a squatter who presides over an eyesore, but little is permanent on Virginia Key. Come the next hurricane, and there will be no sign that the place ever existed.

A darling of Virginia Key whom no one disagrees about is Flipper. The Miami Seaquarium, home to the bottlenose dolphins that have become synonymous with Miami, is an attraction that brings in huge numbers of visitors.

ACCESS: From the north, exit I–95 onto the Rickenbacker Causeway, where I–95 ends and turns into US 1. Virginia Key is the first island you drive onto, and the beach road is opposite the entrance to the Miami Seaquarium.

From the south, follow US 1 north until just before it merges with I–95, then follow the signs for the Rickenbacker Causeway.

PARKING: Multiple parking lots.

HOURS/FEES: 8:00 A.M.–sunset; city of Miami residents $3.00, walk-in $1.00; nonresidents $5.00, walk-in $3.00.

AMENITIES: Rest rooms, showers, lifeguards, picnic tables, grills.

ACTIVITIES: Wading, sunbathing, swimming, picnicking, sailboarding.

FOR MORE INFORMATION: Virginia Key Beach (305) 361–2749.

Crandon Park Beach

The 2-mile beach at Crandon Park is the crown jewel of Miami's beaches, and has been so for more than a half century. Despite having been hit hard by Hurricane Andrew in 1992, the park rebounded quickly and is once again in top form. It fared relatively well compared to the devastation that occurred just to the south at Cape Florida, with most damage done to facilities, not to vegetation. The beach almost always ranks in the top ten of the nation, and millions of people use it each year. An offshore sandbar protects the beach from surf, creating something of a calm lagoon inside of it for people to swim. Many people venture out to the sandbar, which is accessible at low tide by wading. The beach is well patrolled, with thirteen lifeguard towers set out every 150 yards. It's enormously wide. Everything about Crandon Park is spacious, in fact, with a parking area that holds more than 3,000 vehicles.

Another bonus to Crandon is that it's virtually impossible to run out of things to do. The park occupies a great deal of Key Biscayne and includes a full-service marina, a tennis center, restaurants, and a golf course. At the north end of the beach is the sailboarding area, which was developed around the time Virginia Key Beach was closed. Now that Virginia Key Beach is in operation again, there are two fantastic sailboarding beaches in this area. A winding concrete sidewalk connects the beach from end to end, which inline and longboard skaters cruise. In the middle of the vast parking lot is a track oval, ostensibly for high school track meets.

Windsurfing off Crandon Park Beach.

The fine white sand of the beach is as natural and pristine as can be, and with the palm trees swaying in the breeze it's definitely a large chunk of paradise. Crandon is a very timeless place: If you look at pictures from twenty, thirty, fifty years ago, it still looks like that same lazy dream. The park used to all be owned by the Matheson family, one of the great pioneering families of Miami, who also owned the beautiful strip of forest on the mainland side of Biscayne Bay that came to be Matheson Hammock. They were responsible for the planting of the hurricane-resistant coconut palms that dominate Crandon Park, back when they ran it as a coconut plantation. The true beauty of the park is that because it's so large, it's not hemmed in by adjacent development. If you start at the south end and walk north, all you have before you is endless sand and the aqua-blue Atlantic.

ACCESS: From the north, exit I–95 onto the Rickenbacker Causeway, where I–95 ends and turns into US 1. Cross the causeway to Virginia

Key, go past the Seaquarium, cross the next causeway and you will be on Key Biscayne. Crandon Park is 2 miles ahead on your left.

From the south, follow US 1 north until just before it merges with I–95, then follow the signs for the Rickenbacker Causeway and Key Biscayne.

PARKING: Multiple parking lots.

HOURS/FEES: 8:00 A.M.–7:00 P.M.; $3.50 per vehicle.

AMENITIES: Rest rooms, showers, lifeguards, picnic tables, grills, tennis center, golf course, track, visitor center, food concessions, restaurants, marina.

ACTIVITIES: Swimming, wading, picnicking, sailboarding, volleyball, golf, tennis, in-line and longboard skating.

FOR MORE INFORMATION: Crandon Park Beach (305) 361–7385.

Cape Florida/Bill Baggs State Park

At the southern tip of Key Biscayne lies this lovely state park, presided over by one of the most historic lighthouses in Florida, the Cape Florida Lighthouse. In 1835, after a Seminole Indian attack to the north, the entire Miami area was abandoned by the fledgling pioneers. The refugees gathered at the Cape Florida Lighthouse for protection. Soon they fled for Key West. After begrudgingly returning to the lighthouse a few months later, the keeper was given three guards to protect him. One day he sailed for Key West with one of the men to restock on supplies, and the increasingly angry Seminole took advantage by launching an attack on the light. Closing in on the facility, the Seminole set fire to the door and sent the two remaining protectors fleeing to a ledge on top to escape the smoke. One of the men was killed; the other had his feet riddled with bullets, but bravely hung on. Finally the man threw a keg of gunpowder onto the stairs, hoping to blow himself up. Instead, the blast destroyed the stairway and put out the fire, saving him. He played dead until the Seminole left, and was rescued the next day by a U.S. Navy schooner.

Hurricane Andrew walloped the park in 1992. The lighthouse and keeper's dwelling fared okay, but the Australian pines that made up much of the park's vegetation were flattened. This nonnative species has a very shallow root system and does not weather storms well, leaving park workers with a cleanup

Cape Florida Lighthouse.

nightmare. A silver lining appeared in the end, however, because the vegetation has been replanted with native species, and the park looks far more like it did in centuries past. In addition, the lighthouse got a complete makeover in the last few years; tours are running again at 10:00 A.M. and 1:00 P.M. every day.

The park is a draw both from land and by sea, since overnight boat camping is allowed in No Name Harbor. A ship's store sells various nautical items, bait, and tackle, and provides the use of washers, dryers, and showers. The beach extends for more than a mile, and it's wonderful. The same natural sand that is abundance at Crandon Park is available here, and the shallow, clear waters are great for snorkeling, swimming, and wading. On the Biscayne Bay side, fishing is allowed on several platforms. All manner of active recreation is possible, as the concessions rent in-line skates, bicycles, hydrobikes, and kayaks. The Lighthouse Café is the main restaurant of the park, offering quality waterfront dining at a reasonable price. There are miles of paved paths for biking and blading, and even on the busiest of holidays the park seems too far "out there" to draw major crowds. All in all, the overall condition of Cape Florida right now is the best it has ever been, and it was an awfully nice place at its worst.

ACCESS: From the north, exit I–95 onto the Rickenbacker Causeway, where I–95 ends and turns into US 1. Cross the causeway to Virginia Key, cross the next causeway, and you will be on Key Biscayne. Drive past Crandon Park and all the way to the southern tip of the key to the park entrance.

From the south in Miami, follow US 1 north until just before it merges with I–95, then follow the signs for the Rickenbacker Causeway and Key Biscayne.

PARKING: Free lots.

HOURS/FEES: 8:00 A.M.–sunset; $1.00 per hiker or biker, $2.00 per single-occupant vehicle, $4.00 per vehicle with two to eight passengers.

AMENITIES: Rest rooms, showers, lifeguards, picnic tables, grills, eighteen covered pavilions, restaurant, ship's store, kayak/bike/in-line skate rental concession, boat harbor.

ACTIVITIES: Lighthouse tours, snorkeling, wading, sunbathing, swimming, picnicking, fishing, in-line skating, kayaking, bicycling.

FOR MORE INFORMATION: Cape Florida/Bill Baggs State Recreation Area (305) 361–5811.

Matheson Hammock Beach Park

The only beach located on the mainland side of Biscayne Bay, the atoll at Matheson Hammock is artificial but has been in existence for so long that it seems natural. The beach wraps around the human-made atoll pool, which has an outlet to Biscayne Bay that flushes clean water in and out with the tide. Coconut palms provide shade across the beach, and families play with their children in the shallow waters of the pool. Between the beach and the parking lot is the Redfish Grill, a restaurant housed in a gorgeous historic coral rock building surrounded by beautiful landscaping. It's open from 5:00 to 10:00 every evening, and is run by the same people who run one of the best restaurants in Coral Gables, Christy's.

Because Miami Beach and Key Biscayne can be such a long haul through nightmarish traffic for residents of South Miami, Matheson Hammock is a great alternative much closer to home. The park was built by the Civilian Conservation Corps in the 1930s, one of the many visionary New Deal projects that have endured so well over the years. Away from the beach, there's a full-service marina and hiking trails through the lush subtropical hammock of mastic, ironwood, ficus, pigeon plum, and magnificent live oaks. Don't be surprised if you see a giant iguana lurking about, because a feral colony has established itself at neighboring Fairchild Tropical Gardens and throughout this area. They occasionally fall out of ficus trees while sleeping; the crash of one of these 3-foot-long behemoths can be quite startling.

ACCESS: From US 1 or SR 826/Palmetto Expressway, go east on North Kendall Drive (Southwest 88th Street) until it dead-ends at Cutler Drive. Turn right and go 0.5 mile on Cutler. The entrance will be on your left.

PARKING: Large parking lots.

HOURS/FEES: 6:00 A.M.–sunset; $3.50 per vehicle.

AMENITIES: Rest rooms, showers, lifeguards, picnic tables, grills, restaurant.

ACTIVITIES: Sunbathing, swimming, picnicking, dining, hiking, in-line skating, bicycling.

FOR MORE INFORMATION: Matheson Hammock Beach Park (305) 667–3035.

Biscayne National Park

Actual sand beaches are a little hard to come by on the keys of this national park, but they more than make up for it in their beautiful, clear waters and wild emptiness. Though overlooked by many boaters in favor of destinations in the Florida Keys from Key Largo down to Key West, these keys give an impression of what the whole stretch could have been like had someone long ago declared the entire length a national park. Instead, the Florida Keys have been diminished under the weight of unbridled commercialism, and the only federal parks are keys with no road access at the extreme ends: Biscayne National Park and Dry Tortugas National Park.

A park concession boat runs from Convoy Point out to the keys. The concession also includes a group of dive boats and a glass-bottomed boat, and the scuba diving is as fantastic as anywhere to the south. The park's legendary Wall Dive drops from 70 to 110 feet and is claimed to be the only true wall dive in the continental United States. Elkhorn coral abounds. Because only one commercial dive operator is allowed to operate in the park, the reefs have stayed far more pristine than almost anywhere else in the Florida Keys.

The bay side of Elliott Key features some lovely sand beaches, and a 7-mile nature trail runs the entire length of the island. At the north end of the chain, the Ragged Keys—just called the Raggedies by locals—are a great place to poke around in a sea kayak. There's a campground in the middle of Elliott Key and a campground on Boca Chita Key of the Ragged Keys. It's hard to explore this area without the Steely Dan song "Dr. Wu" drifting through your head—"Biscayne Bay, where the Cuban gentlemen sleep all day." You feel like sleeping all day beside these glorious waters, too.

ACCESS: From the Florida Turnpike Extension, take exit 2 onto Campbell Drive, turn left and (east) to Kingman, turn right (south) onto Southwest 328th Street/Canal Drive, then turn left and drive 6 miles east to the end.

From US 1 South, turn left onto Southwest 328th Street/Canal Drive and continue 6 miles east to the end. The Biscayne National Park Visitor Center and park concessions will be on your left at Convoy Point. Just across a small inlet is Homestead Bayfront Park and Marina, a county park and launching site for private boats.

PARKING: Parking lots at the Convoy Point Visitor Center or Homestead Bayfront Park.

HOURS/FEES: Biscayne National Park Visitor Center 8:30 A.M.–5:30 P.M., free; round-trip boat shuttle to Elliott Key $21.00; snorkel package $27.95, two-tank scuba diving $45.00; Homestead Bayfront Park sunrise–sunset, free.

AMENITIES: Visitor center and diving/snorkeling/kayak concession on the mainland; campgrounds, rest rooms, picnic tables, boat docks on Elliott Key and Boca Chita Key; full-service marina and rest rooms, showers, picnic area at Bayfront Park.

ACTIVITIES: Scuba diving, snorkeling, kayaking, hiking, camping, boating.

FOR MORE INFORMATION: Biscayne National Park (305) 230–7275; www.nps.gov/bisc.

Divers Unlimited—Biscayne National Underwater Park (305) 230–1100.

Biscayne Bay.

The South Beach Scene

All manner of cafes, restaurants, bars, and shops fill the blocks of Collins and Washington Avenues on South Beach in Miami, and there's a cool funky element to most of it rather than the upscale trendiness you might expect. Actually, the schizophrenia on South Beach—*glamorous/exclusive* on the one hand, *a place for everyone* on the other—is literally a night-and-day thing. By day there are great expanses of public beach available to the masses, and every level of support network for the beach life. From the most expensive of art deco hotels to cheap eateries and postcard shops, the place hums with tanned flesh and energy. By night the clubs on Washington Avenue start pumping their dance beats, and a whole different crowd of revelers from inland spills out to the beach and dances until four o'clock in the morning.

Because clubs are necessarily confined spaces, trendy ones like Warsaw, Bash, and Liquid are selective about who they let in on weekends, to make sure they maintain their image as hangouts of the beautiful and fabulous. (Actually it's something of a wonder that Patsy and Eddie, those two drippingly sarcastic fashion mavens of the BBC's *Absolutely Fabulous*, never did an episode here.) Your best bet for beating out the throngs of fashion-impaired hopefuls is to comb thrift stores for the most outrageously bright 1970s polyester, and match it with thick fake fur hats and/or coats. If it works in New York and London, believe me, it works in South Beach. You just have to strip as soon as you're inside so you don't sweat to death. Celebrity owners like Prince and Madonna make the clubs even more of a draw, because of the chance of seeing them or some of their Hollywood friends on any given night. Just finding parking on weekend nights can rank you as part of an exclusive set.

Walking the beach at night on South Beach is a wonderful experience. It's reasonably safe and quiet, and the view of the lit-up deco hotels is gorgeous. You can walk all the way down to the jetty at Government Cut and see what the fishermen are catching off the rocks. Don't even be surprised if you see a creature from the black lagoon emerge from the water; it may be just a diver who's been foraging among the rocks for lobster. Sometimes a beach walk is the best way to sober up from a night of excess, and there are plenty of people who have watched the sun rise on South Beach after a night of Dionysian reveling.

Region 9

The Florida Keys are not where people generally go with beaches in mind, though they do boast at least one of the finer strands in the state. It's the water that surrounds the threadbare outcroppings that's the attraction. On the Atlantic side you have more than 100 miles of beautiful coral reefs just offshore, and in the shallows of Florida Bay you have some of the best flats fishing in the United States.

Rare pink flamingos on Key West.

Cannon Beach at John Pennekamp State Park is an artificial one tucked up in the mangrove lagoons, but seems perfectly natural and offers nice snorkeling. Bahia Honda State Park has been rated the best in the nation, with hundreds of acres of shallow, clear waters and loads of room to wander. Down in Key West there is County Beach and Fort Zachary Taylor, though the main tourist hangout is Mallory Square and the ritual watching of the sunset. There are a number of interesting cultural attractions in Key West, including Audubon House and the old home of Ernest Hemingway. Sixty miles across the Gulf of Mexico from Key West is Dry Tortugas National Park, a remote, tiny group of islands that have great waters for diving.

Between Key Largo and Key West there are many state parks, gardens, and historic sites, every one of them worth a visit. Lignumvitae Key and its old Matheson House is one of these, with hardwood forest that you won't find anywhere else in the Keys. Looe Key is an offshore reef down near Big Pine Key that is probably the most colorful dive in the Keys, and is shallow enough to snorkel. Key lime pie is a dessert no Keys visit is complete without, though quality varies widely for something that's so simple to prepare: Mix ½ cup key lime juice, 4 egg yolks, and 8 ounces sweetened condensed milk, pour into a graham cracker crust, and refrigerate.

Access

Take US 1 south from Miami to the Florida Keys.

Beaches

Cannon Beach/John Pennekamp State Park
Bahia Honda State Park
Fort Zachary Taylor
County Beach/Key West
Dry Tortugas National Park

Camping

John Pennekamp State Park—(305) 451–1202. There are forty-seven sites found tucked between a mangrove forest and a tidal creek. Each site comes with a picnic table, fire ring, water spigot, and electricity. Hot showers are included. Several sites have shade with slight privacy while others have little vegetation. Rates are $22 per night. There is also a youth campground that rents for $2.00–3.00 per person per night, accommodating up to twenty-four people.

Bahia Honda State Park—(305) 872–2353. Three separate campgrounds with eighty sites total. The Buttonwood site, with forty-eight spaces, is the best for RVs, with water and electric hookups at every site. Base rates are $19 per night. Six boat-accessible cabins are available with central air and heat, a deck with a picnic table, grill, and outside shower; two bedrooms, living room, kitchen/dining room, full bath. The road to the cabins passes under the Bahia Honda Bridge, with only 6 feet, 8 inches of clearance. They run $110 per night from mid-December to mid-September, $85 per night the rest of the year.

Long Key State Park—(305) 664–4815. Scenery is one of the main attractions at Long Key Campground. All sixty tent/RV campsites offer aquamarine ocean views. Australian pines provide a soft bed of needles atop the sandy soil of the shady campground. Base rates are $19 per night.

Boyd Key West Campgrounds—(305) 294–1465, boydscamp@aol.com. Located in Key West, there are 203 sites for tents and RVs. Campfires permitted. Rates are $35–41 for two-person tent sites in the off season, $41–48 in season. Additional for water/electric or sewer hookups. Discounts for spring breakers staying a week.

Garden Key/Dry Tortugas National Park—This primitive campground is located on the same island as Fort Jefferson and is a short walk from the public dock. Eleven individual sites can accommodate up to six people, or three tents each, and are available on a first-come, first-served basis. The camping fee is $3.00 per person, per night. Campsites have picnic tables and grills. Saltwater flush toilets are available at the dock. Campers must bring all supplies, including fresh water, fuel, ice, and food. All trash and garbage must be carried out upon departure.

Other Points of Interest

Lignumvitae Key—(305) 664–9814, near Islamorada. An old homestead of the Matheson family of Miami, the key houses one of the most intact stands of virgin tropical forest in the Keys. Lignumvitae is one of the hardest woods in existence. The Matheson House is the island visitor center; tours of the island cost $1.00. Access is by tour only at 10:00 A.M. and 2:00 P.M. The tour boat leaves from the mainland a half hour earlier.

Indian Key State Historic Site—(305) 664–4815, near Islamorada. A ten-acre island that was the home of Jacob Housman, a legendary wrecker. The town was the original seat of Dade County, and was burned to the ground by Seminole warriors on August 7, 1840, killing botanist Dr. Henry Perrine and his family.

National Key Deer Refuge—(305) 872–2239, Big Pine Key. A protected zone for the runt-sized Key deer, a tiny white-tailed deer known nowhere else. About 400 remain in a fragile balance, reproducing at about the same rate they get hit by cars.

Hemingway Home and Museum—(305) 294–1575, Key West. The home of the legendary "Papa," a Spanish colonial structure full of artifacts from Ernest Hemingway's adventures around the world.

Audubon House and Gardens—(305) 294–2116, Key West. The home of the great conservationist and painter James J. Audubon, restored and furnished with antiques from the 1700s and 1800s.

Mallory Square—Key West. The famous gathering place for the ritual watching of the sunset every evening. Eclectic mix of personalities and performers.

Great blue heron.

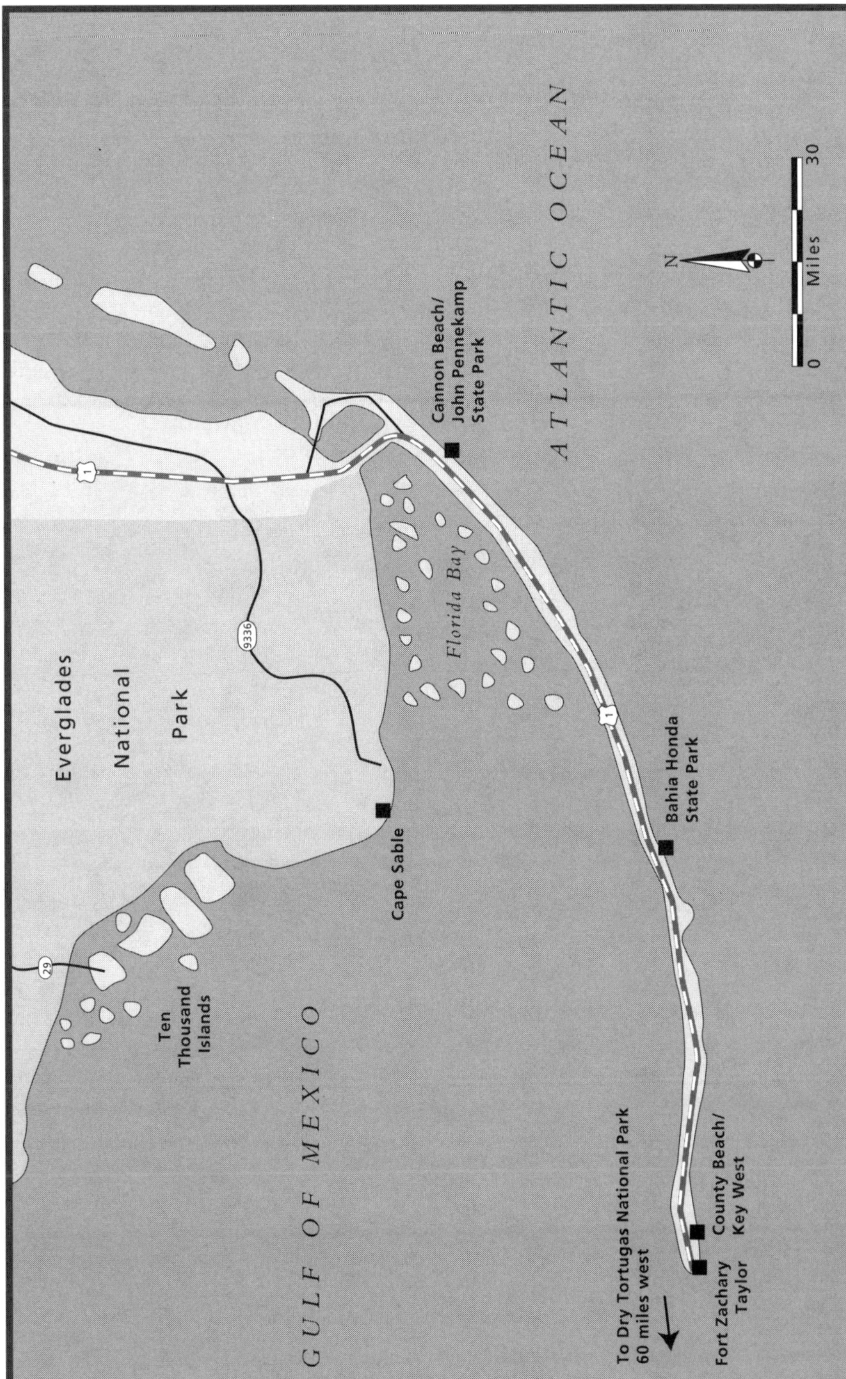

Everglades
National
Park
Cannon Beach/
John Pennekamp
State Park
ATLANTIC OCEAN
N
0
Miles
30
Florida Bay
9336
1
29
Cape Sable
Bahia Honda
State Park
Ten
Thousand
Islands
GULF OF MEXICO
To Dry Tortugas National Park
60 miles west
County Beach/
Key West
Fort Zachary
Taylor

Cannon Beach/John Pennekamp State Park

Not a lot of people are aware of Cannon Beach at Pennekamp State Park, but it is one of the nicest beaches in the Florida Keys. Granted, there's not a great deal of competition since there are so few beaches on this long series of lime rock outcroppings, but it's a very fine place to spend a day in the sun and enjoy some snorkeling. It has an advantage over its competitors because it's an artificial, trucked-in sand beach, though it blends in well with the surroundings.

Pennekamp is primarily known for its underwater allure, and was designed as the first underwater state park in the United States. The boundaries, encompassing 70 square miles, were set up to protect some of the only coral reef that exists in the continental United States. The park also contains vast seagrass beds and mangrove forests, crucial to providing a haven for

John Pennekamp State Park.

young sea life. Dive boats go out several times a day, and some of the more beautiful dives in the park include French, Molasses, and Carysfort Reefs. An unusual attraction is the *Christ of the Abyss* statue, which is located in the Key Largo Dry Rocks area in water shallow enough to snorkel.

On the mainland, long boardwalks lead through mangrove forests where you can see egrets, cormorants, herons, and other bird life. The visitor center has an impressive 30,000-gallon saltwater aquarium that showcases a wide variety of the marine life of the park. Kayak and sailboat rentals are available for meandering through the lagoons and near-shore waters.

The beach is found out toward the northwest corner of the accessible mainland areas, and is a lovely little piece of deep, grainy sand in a part of the world that doesn't feature much of the stuff. Coconut palms dot the beach, and the clear, shallow water of the lagoon lets snorkelers view a replica of a shipwreck, replete with cannons. The shipwreck attracts plenty of marine life, so it's a budget alternative to going out on one of the boats to the coral reefs.

ACCESS: Head south on US 1 from Miami. Upon reaching Key Largo, proceed 3 miles south to John Pennekamp State Park. The entrance will be on your left at Mile Marker 102.5.

Coming up from Key West, look for the mile marker once you're on Key Largo. Ask for directions at the entrance booth to Cannon Beach.

PARKING: Free lots.

HOURS/FEES: 8:00 A.M.–sunset; $1.00 per hiker or biker, $2.00 per single-occupant vehicle, $4.00 per vehicle with two to eight passengers.

AMENITIES: Rest rooms, showers, lifeguards, picnic tables, grills, visitor center with 30,000-gallon saltwater aquarium, marina, dive charters, kayak/sailboat rentals, boat ramp.

ACTIVITIES: Snorkeling, scuba diving, sunbathing, swimming, picnicking, hiking, kayaking, sailing, bicycling, glass-bottomed boat tours.

FOR MORE INFORMATION: John Pennekamp State Park (305) 451–1621.

Bahia Honda State Park

With the old, desolate beauty of the Keys disappearing more and more behind development, places like Bahia Honda give you an appreciation for what most of it used to be like. The tropical hardwood hammock includes rare trees like yellow satinwood and manchineel, the latter of which is one of the most deadly trees of the Caribbean. A brush against a manchineel tree will set off an allergic reaction that makes the worst case of poison ivy seem like nothing. Sitting under manchineel in a rainstorm can leave you blistered all over. Fortunately, there are only one or two in the park, and inadvertent exposure to them is virtually impossible. Most of the eighty sites in the campgrounds are located within the lush hammock, the majority by the ocean and others on the Florida Bay side. Cabins are also available in the park, but usually require reservations in advance. The beach wraps from the Atlantic side around to Florida Bay, with endless, clear, shimmering waters stretching out before you. You can wade out for hundreds of yards and only be in waist-deep water.

The Seven Mile Bridge passes over the south tip of the park, and adjacent to it are the remains of the old railroad bridge that Henry Flagler built. The Bahia Honda Bridge was an engineering marvel that endured three hurricanes during its construction, and spanned 2 miles over the deepest cut and strongest currents of the Keys. The bridge—and the railroad service in the Keys—was shattered forever by the terrifyingly powerful storm of the century, the 1935 hurricane.

Kayaks can be rented in the park, and make a great way to explore the surrounding flats, especially if you bring a mask and snorkel. There are few other beaches in Florida of such simple Caribbean beauty as Bahia Honda, and it's a lot cheaper than an island vacation.

ACCESS: As you head south on US 1 in the Florida Keys, the park is 12 miles south of Marathon at Mile Marker 36.5, just before the Seven Mile Bridge. Coming up from Key West, cross the Seven Mile Bridge and you're there.

PARKING: Free lots.

HOURS/FEES: 8:00 A.M.–sunset; $1.00 per hiker or biker, $2.00 per single-occupant vehicle, $4.00 per vehicle with up to eight passengers.

AMENITIES: Rest rooms, showers, lifeguards, picnic tables, grills, kayak rentals, two boat ramps, campground, cabins.

ACTIVITIES: Snorkeling, sunbathing, swimming, wading, picnicking, hiking, kayaking, bicycling, fishing.

FOR MORE INFORMATION: Bahia Honda State Park (305) 872–2353.

Fort Zachary Taylor

A pretty human-made beach graces the ocean in front of this historic fort, with beautiful views of the fabled Key West sunsets. Offshore there are some rock piles that attract fish and offer good snorkeling. When construction began in 1845, the fort was at the water's edge, but over time it became landlocked. Key West was the lone thriving settlement of South Florida in the nineteenth century, and remained so all the way up until the development of Miami. Fort Zachary Taylor was meant to secure Key West against invasion from all quarters, but proved most useful to the Union during the Civil War. The Union seized the fort before the war broke out, and along with their control over the entrance to Tampa Bay and their fairly rapid capture of Fort Clinch, they crippled the Confederate supply routes in Florida.

The greatest worries of nineteenth-century sailors were wreckers and pirates. The two groups were indistinguishable to some, though wreckers were supposed to be those who simply preyed on the misfortunes of others by salvaging the cargo of wrecks, whereas pirates actively caused the misfortune. Though the reefs of the Keys were dangerous enough to wreck ships without any assistance, many captains believed that wreckers were in cahoots with lighthouse keepers. The theory was that the lighthouse keepers dimmed the light at important moments, causing ships to go on to the rocks. Before you knew it, at least one, if not a half dozen wreckers, would be out at the wrecked ship offering their services. The rough and raucous range of characters who made their living at wrecking was a defining part of Key West culture.

ACCESS: In Key West, the fort is at the end of Southard Street on Truman Annex.

PARKING: Free lots.

HOURS/FEES: 8:00 A.M.–sunset; $1.00 per hiker or biker, $2.00 per single-occupant vehicle, $4.00 per vehicle with two to eight passengers.

AMENITIES: Rest rooms, showers, picnic tables, grills, food concession.

ACTIVITIES: Snorkeling, sunbathing, swimming, picnicking, historic touring, kayaking, fishing.

FOR MORE INFORMATION: Fort Zachary Taylor Historic State Park (305) 292–6713.

County Beach/Key West

The southernmost beach of note in the continental United States, where that grand coastal highway called A1A finally comes to an end, is in Key West. Known to the locals as County Beach, the pier at this park is a beautiful place to watch the sun rise over the bottom of Florida. The swimming is good, there are free tennis courts across the street and volleyball courts on the beach, and there's a bike path for bladers and bikers. It attracts all the usual diverse characters you find in Key West, without ostentatiously being a hangout like the sunset scene at Mallory Square.

Key West's status as an international port for the Caribbean and Latin America has brought all manner of people through it. Over time Key West has retained some of its old character, while dealing with constant redevelopment. The modern Key West definitely is the funky place it is reputed to be, and the historic aspect is surprisingly well maintained. Given the influx of MTV television crews and its ever-growing reputation as a party scene, though, the little town at the tip of Florida is struggling not to become *too* popular.

ACCESS: In Key West, the beach is 0.5 mile west of Smathers Beach on Atlantic Boulevard (A1A) near the south end of White Street.

PARKING: Free street parking and free lots.

HOURS/FEES: 7:30 A.M.–11:30 P.M.; free.

AMENITIES: Volleyball courts, tennis courts, rest rooms, showers, lifeguards, picnic tables, beach cafe.

The beach at sunrise.

ACTIVITIES: Sunbathing, swimming, picnicking, biking, volleyball, tennis.

FOR MORE INFORMATION: Monroe County Parks (305) 295–4385.

Dry Tortugas National Park

Without a doubt, the narrow strips of sand bordering some of the keys in the Dry Tortugas are the most remote beaches you can access anywhere in Florida. Sixty miles west of Key West, they're *out* there. Fort Jefferson is the main land attraction of the Dry Tortugas and is the largest brick fort in the Western Hemisphere. Occupying almost all of Garden Key, it took thirty years to complete after construction began in 1836 and was once used as a federal prison.

There is also a small primitive campground on Garden Key, with thirteen sites accommodating up to six people each. The national park Web site helpfully notes that "because Dry Tortugas National Park can only be reached by boat or seaplane, it is inaccessible to trailers and motorhomes." The waters of the Dry Tortugas are the main attraction, with spectacular diving. No spearfishing or any other fishing except catch-and-release is allowed now in the area, which was one of the first "no-take" marine preserves in the state. These preserves are an important step in restoring overfished areas and important spawning areas, yet have been a struggle to establish, because various fishing lobbies have been unwilling to accept off-limits zones.

While there are saltwater flush toilets and picnic areas, you must bring all your supplies, including an ample supply of fresh water. Nothing is available here and you have to pack all your garbage out with you.

ACCESS: By seaplane, private boat, or ferry from Key West.

PARKING: Vessels may anchor between sunset and sunrise in a designated anchorage area, defined as the area of sand and rubble bottom within 1 nautical mile of the Fort Jefferson harbor light.

HOURS/FEES: This fort is open sunrise–sunset; Loggerhead Key is open for day use only; Bush Key is closed from April through September; Hospital and Long Keys are always closed to visitors. Free.

AMENITIES: Rest rooms, picnic tables, grills, *fresh water.*

ACTIVITIES: Scuba diving, snorkeling, boating, camping, fort touring.

FOR MORE INFORMATION: Dry Tortugas National Park (305) 242–7700; www.nps.gov/drto.

For ferry schedules, prices, and reservations, contact:
Sunny Days (305) 292–6100 or (800) 236–7937.
Yankee Fleet (305) 294–7009 or (800) 634–0939.
Seaplanes of Key West (305) 294–0709 or (800) 950–2FLY.

Hurricanes

Though the Florida Keys have been untroubled by a major hurricane for a long time, this chain of tiny islands has been assaulted in the past by some of the most powerful storms in history. With their low elevations and total exposure, the results have been devastating. The most powerful Atlantic hurricane of the twentieth century barreled through the upper Keys in 1935, drowning more than 400 people, many of them World War I veterans who were working on a New Deal project to build the Keys highway. The train that was supposed to evacuate them was washed off the track on its way.

The Alligator Reef lighthouse keeper recalled, "I looked up and there was a wave coming at me that I fully believe was 90 feet high. I barely made it to grab hold of the ladder when it broke over the light, and how I held on and why I wasn't drowned, I can't say."

Winds roared over 200 miles per hour, so great there wasn't anything capable of measuring them. My grandmother wrote of the eye of the storm, based on one family's description:

> There was the roar of the wind, a savage, brutal beast of a wind, louder than a locomotive right on top of you. Suddenly the wind slacked, failed, gasped fitfully. It was like a great animal dying, gasping for breath. There were two minutes of that lull. "Daddy," said one child, "when I breathe I don't get any air! My lungs get no good of it!" They were in the eye of the storm. The captain later found his barometer stuck at 26.55. All they knew then was that if the lull had been drawn out to three minutes, they felt they would have strangled for want of air.

Floridians in recent years have rashly begun to underestimate hurricanes, because so few aside from Andrew in 1992 have had a major impact. If ever a Class 5 behemoth like the 1935 hurricane hits again, it will be a natural disaster the likes of which our nation has rarely seen.

Index

A

A. E. "Beanie" Backus Gallery, 62
Ah-Tha-Ki Museum, 131
Amelia Island, 1
Amelia Island Museum of History, 2–3, 18
Amelia Island State Park, 8
American Beach, 1, 7–8
American Beach for African Americans, An, 7
Anastasia limestone, 98
Anastasia State Park, 19, 21, 23
Andersen, Lisa, 31
Apollo Beach, 41, 48–49
Archie Carr National Wildlife Refuge, 70
Audubon House and Gardens, 164, 166
Aury, Luis, 18
Australian pine, xv, 127, 129, 156, 158
Avalon, 74–75

B

Baal, Robert, 111
Bahia Honda Bridge, 170
Bahia Honda State Park, 164, 165, 170–71
Baltimore Orioles Spring Training Center, 131
Barton Park, 118
Bass Museum, 148
Bathtub Reef Beach, 90–92
Beachfest, 53
Bella Vista plantation, 27
Benny's, 117
Bethune, Mary McLeod, 7, 39–40
Bethune Beach Park, 39, 47
Betsch, MaVynne, 7
Bicentennial Park, 31–32
Big Talbot Island State Park, 9–10
Bike Week, 20
Bill Baggs State Park, 156–58
Billie Swamp Safari, 131
birding, 11, 17, 74
Biscayne National Park, 147, 160–61
Black Heritage Trail, 3
blacks, 7, 39
"Bloody Matanzas," 25
Blowhole, 23
Blowing Rocks Preserve, 98
Boca Chita Key Campground, 147
Boca Raton, 104
Body Heat, 117
bottlenose dolphins, 153
Boyd Key West Campgrounds, 165
Boynton Public Beach, 119
Brevard County Museum of History and Natural Science, 43
Brevard Zoo, 61

Briny Breezes, 103–4
Bullet, The, 19

C

Canaveral National Seashore, 41–42, 48–51
Canaveral Pier, 53–54
Cannon Beach, 168–69
Cape Florida, 156–58
Cape Florida Lighthouse, 156–58
Carlin Park, 103, 108–9
Carr, Archie, 70
Casements Cultural Center, The, 21, 30
Castillo de San Marcos, 19, 21
casuarina, xv, 127, 129, 156, 158
Chastain Beach, 92
Cherie Down Park, 52
Christ of the Abyss, 169
Civil War, 6, 18, 171
Cocoa Beach, 53–54
Cocoa Beach Surfing School, 43
Coco's Café, 138
Colee family, 127
Colonnades Hotel, 113
Conkey, Joe, 104
coquina rock, xv, 19, 27, 30, 55
Coral Cove Beach, 99
County Beach, 172–73
Crandon Park Beach, 154–56
Cross, Bunky, 14
Cummer Museum of Art and Gardens, 3

D

Daytona Beach, 19–20, 32–34
Daytona Beach Boardwalk, 32
Deerfield Beach, 133–34
Deerfield Beach Art Show, 134
Deerfield Beach Pier, 133
Delray Beach, 104, 120–21
Dickinson, Jonathan, 49, 78, 100–101
diving, 143, 160, 168–69, 174
Dodgertown, 62
dolphins, bottlenose, 153
Dreher Park Zoo, 105
Dry Tortugas National Park, 164, 165, 174

E

Easterlin Park, 130
Easter Surfing Festival, 53
Eldora State House, 48–49
elkhorn coral, 160
Elliott Key Campground, 147
Elliott Museum, 83, 89

F

Fairchild Tropical Garden, 148, 159
Fernandina, 1
First Peak, 59
Flagler, Henry, 30
Flagler Beach, 29–30
Flagler Beach Pier, 21
Flagler Museum, 106
Flamingo Gardens and Arboretum, 131

Flipper, 153
Florida East Coast Railroad, 30
Florida Oceanographic Society, 83, 89
Fonda, Peter, 1
Fort Caroline National Memorial, 3
Fort Castillo de San Marcos, 19, 21
Fort Clinch State Park, 1, 2, 5–6, 18, 171
Fort George Island, 12–14
Fort Jefferson, 174
Fort Lauderdale, 127
Fort Lauderdale Beach, 127, 136–38
Fort Matanzas National Monument, 19, 25–26
Fort Pierce Inlet State Park, 76–77
Fort Zachary Taylor, 171–72
Frank Butler Park, 24–25
Frederick Douglass Beach, 85
Fruit and Spice Park, 148

G

Gamble Rogers Memorial State Recreation Area, 21, 29–30
Garden Key, 165, 174
Gilbert's Bar House of Refuge, 79, 83, 90
Gold Coast Railroad Museum, The, 148
Gray, Bill, 79
Gray, Herman, 79
Guana River State Park, 15–17
Gulf Stream, 125
Gulfstream Park, 121–22
Gumbo Limbo Nature Center, 106, 123

H

Halifax & St. Johns Railroad, 30
Hamilton, George, 136
Hanna Park, 2, 14–15
Hartley, Bill, 59
Haulover Beach, 142
Hawley Education Center, 98
Hemingway Home and Museum, 164, 166
Hernandez, Joseph, 27
Hillsboro Inlet Lighthouse, 130, 134
Hobe Sound National Wildlife Refuge, 95–96
Hobe Sound Nature Center, 83
Hobe Sound Public Beach, 97
Holeman, Jon, 65
Hollywood Beach, 140–41
Hollywood Boardwalk, 129, 140
Hontoon Island State Park, 43
horseback riding, 8, 85
Hugh Taylor Birch State Park, 130, 135–36
Huguenot Memorial Park, 2, 12–14
Huguenots, French, 25
hurricanes, 175
Hurston, Zora Neale, 99

I

iguanas, 159

IMAX Theater, 131
Indian Key State Historic Site, 165
Indian River Lagoon, 98
Indiatlantic Boardwalk, 65
International Swimming Hall of Fame, 131

J

Jack Island Preserve, 74
Jacksonville Maritime Museum, 3
Jacksonville Museum of Contemporary Art, 3
Jacksonville Zoological Gardens, 3
Jacobs, Bob, 80
Jarmusch, Jim, 59
Jaycee Park, 72
jellyfish, xiii
Jensen Public Beach, 88–89
Jetty Park, 42, 51–52
Jimbo's, 153
Joe's Stone Crab, 147
John D. MacArthur Beach State Park, 111–12
John Pennekamp State Park, 164, 168–69
John U. Lloyd State Park, 138–39
Jonathan Dickinson State Park, 83
Juno Beach Park, 110
Jupiter Island, 81–82
Jupiter Lighthouse, 83, 99

K

Kennedy Space Center, 42, 57
Kessman, Herbert, 104
Key lime pie, 164
Key West, 171, 172–73
KOA Kampground, 61
Kreusler Park, 117–18

L

Labor Day Surfing Festival, 53
Lake Ashby Park, 41
Lake Worth Municipal Beach, 117–18
Lauderdale, William, 127
Lewis, A. L., 7
Lighthouse Café, 158
Lighthouse Point Park, 34–36
Lignumvitae Key, 164, 165
Little Talbot Island State Park, 2, 11–12
Loehr, Greg, 64
Loggerhead Park, 110
Long Key State Park, 165
Long Point Park, 61, 67–68
Looe Key, 164
Lori Wilson Park, 54–55
Loxahatchee River, 105

M

MacArthur, John D., 113
MacArthur Dairy, 111
Mallory Square, 164, 166, 172
Manalapan, 103
Manatee Hammock, 42
manchineel, 170

Mango Festival, 134
Marineland, 21
Marine Life Center, 105
Matheson family, 155
Matheson Hammock Beach Park, 159
Matheson House, 164
McGregor, Gregor, 18
McLarty Treasure Museum, 59, 71
Melbourne, 59
Memorial Art Center and Gardens, 30
Merritt Island National Wildlife Refuge, 43
Metrozoo, 148
Miami Seaquarium, 147, 153
Monkey Jungle, 148
Monster Hole, 71
Morikami Museum and Japanese Gardens, 106
Mosquito Inlet Lighthouse, 34
motorcycles, 20
mountain biking, 14
Munro, Mimi, 31
Museum of Arts and Sciences, 21
Museum of Discovery and Science, 131
Museum of Science and Space Transit Planetarium, 148

N

Nantwich, 101
Nassau Sound, 1
National Key Deer Refuge, 166
Navy SEALs, 60
New Smyrna Beach, 7, 39
New York Mets Spring Training, 83
North Beach Park, 139–40
North Peninsula State Recreation Area, 31
North Shore Open Space Park, 150
nudity, xiv, 50, 96, 129, 142

O

Oceanfront Park, 30–31
Ocean Reef Park, 113
Ocean Ridge Hammock Park, 119
Old Fernandina, 18
Olds, Ransom, 19
Oleta River State Park, 147
Ormond Beach, 19
Ormond Hotel, 30

P

Parrot Jungle and Gardens, 148
Patrick Air Force Base, 55–56
Peck's Lake, 96
Pelican Beach Park, 64
Pelican Island National Wildlife Refuge, 61, 70
Pepper, Claude, 60
Pepper Beach County Park, 75–76
Perfect Storm, The, 59
Phelts, Marsha Dean, 7
Phipps Ocean Park, 116–17
Pirate, The, 19

Playalinda Beach, 50–51
Pompano Beach, 134–35
Port Canaveral, 51
Portuguese men-of-war, xiii
Propper, Gary, 53

Q

Quiet Waters Park, 130

R

Ragged Keys, 160
"RC's," 59
Redfish Grill, 159
Red Reef Park, 123
Reef Road, 115
Reformation, 100
Reno, Jane Wood, 78–80
Riverbreeze Park, 42
Riviera Beach Municipal Beach, 114
Rockefeller, John D., 30
Rocks, The, 19, 27–29

S

safety, xiii–xiv
sailboarding, 153, 154
Satellite Beach Library, 64
Satellite Beach Skatepark, 61
Savannas Recreation Area, 82
Sayles, John, 1
Scout Island, 68
sea oats, xiv–xv
Seaside Grill, 72
Sea Turtle Beach, 88–89
sea turtles, xv, 37, 70, 95, 111
Sebastian Inlet Marina, 61
Sebastian Inlet State Park, 61, 69–72
Seminole Indians, 27, 127, 156
Shakespeare by the Sea, 103, 109
sharks, xiii, 39
shipwrecks, 59, 71, 90, 171
65th Street Beach, 151
Skycoaster, 32
Skyride, 32
Slater, Kelly, 40
Smith, Rick, 143
Smyrna Dunes Park, 45–46
snorkeling, 90–91, 123, 168–69
South Beach, 145, 151–52, 162
South Beach Park, 73–74
South Florida Science Museum, 105
South Inlet Park, 124
South Patrick Resident Association Park, 56
space shuttle launches, 50, 51, 54, 57
Spanish-American War, 18
Spanish House, 67–68
Spessard Holland Golf Course, 66
Spessard Holland Park, 66
Spruce Creek Park, 21
St. Augustine, 19
St. Augustine Lighthouse, 21
St. Lucie Inlet State Preserve, 93–94
Stranger than Paradise, 59
"Stream, The," 125
Stuart Beach, 89–90
submarines, Trident, 51

Sunshine State, 1
surfing, 31, 40, 45, 53, 65, 69, 76

T

Talbot Islands GeoPark, 1
Terramar Visitor Center, 135
Their Eyes Were Watching God, 99
Tokeepeegee Yugnee Park, 130
Tomoka State Park, 21
Tosohatchee State Reserve, 42
"Town of Eight Flags," 18
Treasure Coast, 59
trees, dead, 9–10
Trident submarines, 51
Turtle Creek Beach, 87–88
turtles, sea, xv, 37, 70, 95, 111

U

UDT-Navy SEAL Museum, 60, 62
Ulee's Gold, 1
Underwater Demolition Team, 60, 138
U.S. Astronaut Hall of Fame, 42–43

V

Virginia Key Beach, 153–54
Vizcaya Museum and Gardens, 148

W

Wall Dive, 160
Walton Rocks Beach, 87–88
Washington Oaks State Gardens, 19, 27–29
Where the Boys Are, 136
Wickham Park, 42
windsurfing, 153
Winton, Alexander, 19
Witham, Ross, 37
World War II, 18, 60
wormrock, 91
wreck diving, 143
Wreck Trek, 143

Y

Yulee, David Levy, 1

Z

Zamba, Frieda, 31

About the Author

George Hurchalla inherited his love of Florida's natural beauty and wild places from his grandmother and mother, both of whom worked to enhance and preserve Florida's coastline. Throughout his youth, Hurchalla visited beaches from one end of the state to the other with his family and paddled canoes through the maze of mangrove creeks along the Intracoastal Waterway.

Now a professional photographer and writer, Hurchalla's subjects alternate between mountain sports in Lake Tahoe and wilderness adventures in Florida. His work has been published in *Florida Sportsman*, *Outside*, *Bike*, *Paddler*, *Miami Herald*, *Florida Living*, and *Florida Water*. In 2001 Hurchalla released *Backcountry Snowboarding in the Northern Sierras*, a CD-ROM guidebook.

PHOTO: JAMES HURCHALLA